# SEA OVER BOW

# SEA OVER BOW

## A NORTH ATLANTIC CROSSING

*Linda Kenyon*

EDITIONS

Cover design by Doowah Design.
Photo of Linda Kenyon by Chris Hatton.

This book was printed on Ancient Forest Friendly paper.
Printed and bound in Canada.

We acknowledge the support of the Canada Council for the Arts and the Manitoba Arts Council for our publishing program.

Library and Archives Canada Cataloguing in Publication

Kenyon, Linda J. (Linda Jean), 1956-, author
    Sea over bow : a North Atlantic crossing / Linda Kenyon.

Issued in print and electronic formats.
ISBN 978-1-77324-040-4 (softcover).--ISBN 978-1-77324-041-1 (EPUB)

    1. Kenyon, Linda J. (Linda Jean), 1956- --Travel--North Atlantic Ocean. 2. Transatlantic voyages. 3. Sailing--North Atlantic Ocean. 4. Sailors--Canada--Biography. 5. Authors, Canadian (English)--Biography. I. Title.

G530.K35K46 2018          910.9163'1          C2018-905150-7
                                               C2018-905151-5

Signature Editions
P.O. Box 206, RPO Corydon, Winnipeg, Manitoba, R3M 3S7
www.signature-editions.com

*Send me out into another life*
*lord because this one is growing faint*
*I do not think it goes all the way*

—W.S. Merwin

*Prologue*

I am braced in the companionway with just my head and shoulders above deck, holding on so tightly my fingernails will leave marks in the wood. The cockpit enclosure protects me from the wind, which howls through the rigging. But it doesn't protect me from the salt spray, not entirely. Water drips through every little gap in the canvas, around the zippers, between the snaps. A wave breaks over the boat, drenching the cockpit completely, and for a minute I can't see anything through the plastic windows. Then they clear.

I'm not sure which is better, seeing or not seeing.

When we're in a trough, all I can see is a wall of water moving towards us. It's hard to tell how big the waves are. Three metres? Four? Sometimes they just lift us up, pass beneath the boat, set us back down more or less gently. When we're on the crest of a wave, all I see is confusion in every direction, waves crashing into each other sending plumes of salt spray into the air. Sometimes a wave breaks beside the boat and we slew as the water boils around us. It's worse when a wave slams against the side with a heavy thud and the boat rolls sharply, then rights itself.

But not as bad as when a wave breaks right over us with a mighty crash. The boat shudders sickeningly, then is still for a moment, and water pours out through the scuppers. Then it all starts again.

I look down through the companionway. Chris is stretched out on the starboard settee, asleep, I think. How is that possible? His face is relaxed, peaceful almost, his greying hair a tousled mess. Who is this man? And what am I doing here? I could be back at my condo right now, sitting beside the fire, a glass of wine in hand, a big fat book open on my lap.

What am I doing?

# NO TURNING BACK

*May 22*

~~~~~

*Day 1*

We haven't set the anchor properly, just dropped it over the side to keep us more or less in the same place while Chris finishes scrubbing the bottom. He couldn't see the hull clearly in the murky waters of English Harbour and wants it to be as smooth and clean as possible for the crossing—a dirty bottom can take up to a knot off our speed, he's mentioned several times. So although technically we're underway, we've pulled into a shallow, sandy bay on the southeastern tip of Antigua while he gives the hull one more going over. Perhaps he's a little more apprehensive about the crossing than he lets on.

I'm down below making lunch and keeping an eye on a tall palm tree on shore, making sure we don't drift too far. I slice into a red pepper, holding it over the sink to catch the drips, core it, scrape out the seeds, dice it into a bowl, not the pottery bowl I usually make salads in—that's tucked away in a sweater somewhere. I'm using a stainless steel bowl, part of a nested set I use when we're underway. They're absolutely indestructible. At least they have been so far.

But compared to what we're about to do, the trip from Lake Erie to Antigua was a Sunday afternoon sail. We motored down the Erie Canal, tying up at the end of each day for a good night's sleep, then down the Hudson River to New York City, where we waited for the right weather to set out into the ocean. We hugged the coast from New York to Miami, never out of sight of shore, for the most part, and slipping into the intracoastal waterway, an inland passage running all the way from Norfolk to the Florida Keys, when we needed a break from ocean sailing. From Miami, it was just an overnight sail to the Bahamas, then after an easy sail to the British Virgin Islands, we pretty much island-hopped our way to Antigua.

My dad has been following our progress on a big map he's thumbtacked to the corkboard in Mom's room at the nursing home. Whenever he hears from us, he marks our position with a pushpin, loops a piece of red yarn around it. Dad tells anyone who comes in what we're doing, where we are now, how he would have done it. I can see the personal care worker nodding as she helps Mom onto the commode. Uh huh. Is that right? A little to the left. Joan, I need you to move to the left.

When she's back in her chair, Mom wheels up to the map, leans forward, peers at it.

"Oh my god!" I can hear her saying when she sees we've headed out into the ocean, or "Jesus!" which is kind of funny. We kids were never allowed to take the Lord's name in vain, as she called it. I guess she has a whole lifetime of profanity saved up. And a lot to curse.

Mom was in her mid-sixties when she had a massive stroke. One minute she was passing the Christmas cake and the next the plate clattered to the floor, her arm gone limp and half her face collapsed. She never regained use of her right arm and had only a handful of one-syllable words left to her. Yes. No. I don't know, she would say, when she couldn't find the words she wanted, which was most of the time. I don't care, when she gave up trying. She would lock eyes with you then, try to get you to understand what she was trying to say. And sometimes you could.

One night, when she was having a particularly bad night and we were taking turns sitting with her, I watched her sleeping, reached over and wiped a line of dribble from her chin. It was too much for me. I put my head on my hands on the rail of her bed and let the tears run silently down my cheeks. She couldn't have heard me, but then I felt her hand softly stroking my hair. I looked up and her dark eyes were fixed on me.

"I know," she said quietly. "I know."

"Jesus!" is probably the right response to what we are about to do. When we set out this time, there will be no more island-hopping.

We won't be able to stop until we reach Bermuda, which should take us about ten days. Our plan is to rest there briefly before making the fifteen-day crossing to the Azores.

The magnitude of what I'm doing, what I've done, really began to sink in as we started provisioning for the ocean crossing. Chris, an engineer, has a wealth of theoretical knowledge. He's been reading books about ocean sailing all his life.

"So here's how you do it," he instructed me. "It's roughly 2,300 miles to the Azores, the way we're planning to go. If we make good 100 miles a day, that's twenty-three days at sea. Make it twenty-five. We should count on a storm every five days, easy sailing two days out of five, and rougher weather the other two. So that's five storm days, ten calm days, and ten rough days."

Five storm days, I thought. I can handle that. As long as they're not all in a row. I set up a spreadsheet on my computer, with twenty-five days down the left-hand side and breakfast, lunch, and dinner across the top. I colour-coded the days as *storm*, *calm*, and *rough*, then started plotting out meals. On storm days, we'd have cold cereal for breakfast, soup and cheese and crackers for lunch, canned stew for dinner. Or maybe cheese and crackers again. Calm days were much more fun to plan. I'd bake bread, make chicken cacciatore, meatloaf, shepherd's pie. We'd heat up leftovers on the rougher days, or have pasta and a jar of sauce.

I started my list.

Our freezer is tiny, about the size of two loaves of bread, so I planned to fill it with meat, but there would be canned tuna, lots of it, and chickpeas, for when the meat ran out. The fresh produce would last a couple of weeks at the most, so I added canned vegetables to the list, even though we never eat them. V8, a couple of cases of it, to prevent scurvy. UHT milk, which has a shelf life of six months and doesn't taste too bad when it's really cold. We didn't need butter—Chris had ordered a case of it from Australia before we left. Two dozen eggs, which he had promised would last for a couple of weeks as long as they had never been washed or refrigerated.

Shampoo, toilet paper, soap, paper towels, dish detergent…the list grew longer and longer. And bottled water, lots of it, enough to get us to the Azores, if necessary, if our water tanks sprang a leak. Lots of tea and coffee. And chocolate, of course, for those long night watches.

By the time we scratched off the last item on our list, we'd filled two grocery carts—and that was without the water. The bill was a staggering $2,197.

"Holy cow!" I said.

"Eastern Caribbean dollars," Chris said. He inspected the cash register tape. "That's $1,465 Canadian dollars. About $500 a week. But we bought lots of extra stuff, just in case we're out there longer."

"Holy cow," I said again.

It took us all day to transport our provisions to the boat, one dinghy load at a time, and stow them. By the time we were done, the V-berth was full, four-litre jugs of water bungee-corded along both sides, paper towels and toilet paper wedged between them, fresh produce and eggs carefully arranged in mesh hanging baskets with lots of room to swing. The food lockers were packed tight so nothing would rattle around, cans and heavy things in the lower lockers, lighter things higher up. The cupboards in the galley were carefully stocked with things I'd want to put my hands on quickly—tea, coffee, crackers, ginger snaps to combat sea sickness.

I collapsed on the settee, wiped the sweat off my face with a cool washcloth while Chris listened to Chris Parker on the SSB radio. A sailor himself and a serious student of weather, Chris Parker provides detailed weather forecasts morning and evening. He'd been keeping a careful eye on an early-season hurricane that had just made landfall in the Honduras. It seemed to have petered out, but we wanted to be sure the weather was back to normal before we set out. Chris took off his headphones, shook his head.

"Another day," he said.

One more comfortable night's sleep at anchor, I thought. One more hot pineapple turnover for breakfast at the bakery on shore. One more quick trip to the woman who sells produce outside the gate—maybe she'll have fresh mangoes in the morning.

"Too bad," I said to Chris. "Let's walk over to Falmouth Harbour for one last chocolate martini."

On the way back, we ran into the one-legged beggar who had befriended us. Or we him. I'm not sure which.

He was one of the first people we had met after dropping anchor in English Harbour. He spotted us right away, new people in town, and hopped towards us as fast as he could go.

"Uh-oh," I had said to Chris.

Then he was upon us. He leaned on his crutches, offered Chris his hand, shook it heartily. Wait for it, I thought. And it came. A long story about a man who had promised him work but then didn't show up and maybe he would show up tomorrow but in the meantime could we spare any change?

Chris dug into his pocket. We'd just arrived and didn't have any change yet, so he gave the man a five-dollar bill.

"Thanks, man," he said, and hurried away.

Later that afternoon we saw him sprawled out on the dock, singing to himself, smiling, all worries about work—and his missing leg—clearly forgotten.

The next time we saw him, Chris had a fistful of change ready. He accepted it gratefully—relieved, I think, that he didn't have to come up with another story. And so it went. We saw him pretty much every time we walked over to Falmouth Harbour. He took to greeting us by gently punching our fists rather than shaking hands like he did with the tourists, and Chris would give him whatever change he had in his pocket.

I don't know his story, and I was too shy to ask. He was young, maybe in his early thirties. He wore the same threadbare pants every day, the empty right leg pinned up so it didn't get tangled in his crutches. He was skinny—his pants seemed always on the verge of falling down, and his shirt was always open, exposing his hollow stomach. What happened to your front teeth, I wanted to ask him. They were broken, as though he'd been hit hard in the mouth. How did you lose your leg, I wanted to know. Or maybe I didn't.

That last evening we could tell by his unfocussed grin that he had had a really good day. He punched Chris's hand, punched mine. Chris dug into his pocket and gave him what was left of our Eastern Caribbean money—change, bills, all of it. We aren't planning to keep a ziplock bag of money from every country we visit.

He laughed out loud, then took Chris's hand in his and started singing, not a song so much as a joyful chant. We couldn't understand a word he said. He smiled and sang, kept nodding at me, then at Chris. He took my hand and pressed it into Chris's, put his hands around ours, sang a few more lines, then gave our hands a firm squeeze and released them. He was still smiling and nodding at us as we walked away.

"What just happened?" I asked Chris.

"I think we just got married."

I CHECK THE palm tree. Yep. Still where it was. I can hear the scrunch, scrunch, scrunch of the scrub brush on the bottom of the boat so I know Chris is okay.

A man and a woman appear on the beach. The man points to our boat, shades his eyes with one hand as he studies it. It's an unusual boat for these waters, not a modern fibreglass production boat, but a steel boat built lovingly by hand (not our hands, alas) twenty years ago—thirty if you count from the day Marv started working on it. Marv was an electrician but his real passion was for woodworking.

The first time I climbed down the companionway ladder I couldn't believe my eyes. The boat is fitted with beautiful ash cabinetry, gleaming tongue and groove on the walls, ash boards with teak strips between them on the floor. But the cushions—those would have to go. As would the frying pan full of bolts and washers on the stove. Now we have leather cushions, and the brass lamp above the table is polished until you can see your reflection in it. The tools and fasteners and cable ties and bits of wire have migrated back to the engine room.

But of course the couple on shore can't see any of this. What they see is a sailboat with a pointy bow angling sharply up out of the water. The seas have to be pretty big before waves break over the bow. Our backup anchor hangs off the front of the boat, ready to deploy at a moment's notice, and there are twenty-litre jugs of water and diesel fuel lashed along the side of the deck. A life raft sits prominently on the foredeck, just behind the mast. No one could mistake us for anything but an ocean-going sailboat.

But the most distinctive thing about our boat is the cockpit enclosure. Most sailboats have removable canvas and plastic for protection from the elements, but Chris has designed and built a permanent steel structure with a sturdy Plexiglas windscreen and canvas side curtains that can be completely closed up in bad weather. Unlike a pilothouse, which looks like a cabin plunked down on a sailboat, our enclosure follows the sleek lines of the boat.

Though the couple on shore probably can't see them, the roof above the cockpit is completely covered with solar panels, used to charge a bank of batteries that power the fridge, the lights, all the electronics. Behind the cockpit is a radar arch crowded with antennas, not just for the radar but for the VHF radio, the main GPS, the backup GPS, the satellite phone. There are a couple of compasses up there for good measure, and an orange life ring tied to one side of the radar arch. And a bucket. And a fishing rod. Some nice pieces of rope that might just come in handy sometime.

I chop up a couple of carrots, an onion, toss them into the bowl, open a can of chickpeas, rinse them in as little water as possible, dump them in, add a glug of olive oil, a dash of balsamic vinegar. Hmm, haven't heard any scrubbing for a bit. I wipe my hands on a tea towel, go above deck. Chris is at the stern, hanging from the swim ladder, catching his breath.

"Done!" he says.

"Good timing. Lunch is ready."

I hand him a towel, then go below and bring up the bowl of salad and two forks. We eat on the back deck while Chris dries off. The hills surrounding the bay are a lush green, the sky pale blue, the water a deeper shade of blue but so clear you can see the sandy bottom. I'm tempted to go for a quick swim, but we need to get underway—we'd like to clear the reefs off Barbuda before nightfall.

I stow the lunch things while Chris gets out of his wet bathing suit, then we pull anchor (when will it see the bottom again?) and we're on our way.

"Here, take the helm for a minute," Chris says as we motor out of the little bay. "Steer for the middle of the cut." He goes back and drops the fishing line in the water, puts the rod in the stand at the stern, then comes and takes the wheel. Just as we're entering the cut, the line starts zinging out.

"Fish on," Chris shouts, but he can't go back and land it until we're through the cut. Once we're out in the ocean, he goes back and checks the line.

"Lost it," he says, reeling it in. "Well, lost most of it."

I look back. There's a fish head on the line, a big one, about the size of a dinner plate. The only thing large enough to bite a fish that size in two would be a shark. It must have been a huge one.

"So I guess we won't be doing a lot of swimming out here?"

Chris tosses the fish head in the water.

"Dessert," he says.

"You might have been dessert. And lunch too."

"No, sharks don't come into the shallows. Besides, I would have wrestled it into submission," he says with a grin.

If you can cross an ocean on bravado alone, we've got it made.

OUR FIRST NIGHT at sea is gentle, magical almost. The moon is full, the winds light, the seas calm. We leave a trail of phosphorescence in our wake, a swath of sparkling, blue-green light tracing our path across the dark water.

It seems to take forever to pass Barbuda, the island just north of Antigua. We can hear waves breaking over the reefs along the east side of the island as we ghost along. Sometimes we can actually see them reflected in the light of the moon. We keep checking the charts carefully, confirming our position every fifteen minutes, just to be sure we haven't drifted towards the rocks. They sound so much closer than they are.

We haven't seen another boat since we set sail. This is nothing like our very first night in the ocean.

WE'D BEEN WAITING at anchor behind Sandy Hook, a spit of land just south of New York City, for more than a week, hoping the weather would settle enough for us to set out into the ocean. But we'd woken to thirty-knot winds. Again. The gales of November were setting in. Time to go.

We figured if we hugged the coast, we would be okay. But the wind shifted to the north and the seas built steadily throughout the day, causing the boat to wallow sickeningly as the autopilot struggled to keep up with the following seas. We were making good progress, though. By nightfall, we were approaching Atlantic City.

Chris took the first night watch. We were overtaken by a sailboat—he chatted with the captain for a while—and a freighter passed us far off on our port side. Before going below, Chris pointed out the freighter's lights receding in the distance. Good, I thought. The shipping lanes must be well offshore, like they are in Lake Huron.

I was wrong. There may have been shipping lanes out there somewhere, but closer to shore, it wasn't quite as orderly as all that. As I watched the freighter's lights slowly disappear, I noticed two white lights, one above the other, moving towards us, closing fast.

White over white, I muttered to myself. I grabbed the handy reference card I keep in the cockpit, switched on the flashlight. White over white...oh yeah, towing at night. It was a tugboat coming towards us, probably heading into Atlantic City. I could see that it would pass well ahead of us but I kept my binoculars trained on it until both the tugboat and the barge it was towing were safely past us.

Whew. I lowered my binoculars. Wait, what's that? Two white lights, one above the other, coming out from the coast. Another tugboat, and of course it was coming right for us. Clearly we were passing the entrance to the busy harbour at Atlantic City. But suddenly I could see his starboard running light. He had seen us and was altering course to pass behind us.

This time I didn't lower my binoculars but did a complete 360-degree scan, dividing the horizon into quarters, scanning first in one quarter, then the next. Out of the corner of my eye, I spotted a fishing trawler off our port quarter. Green over white, fishing at night. He was well out to sea and probably out there for the night, but I kept an eye on him anyway in case he decided to come in with his catch.

Nothing off our port bow, nothing off our starboard bow, nothing off our stern — wait, what's that? I peered into the darkness. In the distance, I could just make out a white light flanked by red and green lights. I didn't have to refer to my card. This was bad. If I could see his masthead light and both running lights, he was coming straight towards us. And fast. I checked his position on radar, made a little *x* where he was, checked again in a couple of minutes. He was much closer. Maybe he'd see us and alter course? Nope. I had to think fast.

I picked up the handheld radio. "To the vessel on my stern just south of Atlantic City, this is the sailboat *MonArk*."

There was no response. And the ship had closed by another half mile. I decided to try a new tactic.

"To the ship at —" I gave his longitude and latitude " — this is *MonArk*."

A long pause, then a clipped voice on the radio. "To the vessel hailing, this is the — "

In my nervousness, I missed the name of the ship. I asked if he had me on his radar, and he confirmed somewhat brusquely that he did. Then I asked if he wanted me to maintain my course and speed while he passed me.

Another long pause.

"What kind of vessel are you?" he asked.

"A forty-three-foot sailboat," I replied. "Under sail," I added, in case he wasn't familiar with the rules of the road.

An even longer pause, then he said, "I'll alter course to pass you on your starboard side."

He changed his heading slightly and I found myself looking at the port side of a huge ocean freighter. What is he doing not a mile and a half offshore? I watched in wonder as he passed beside us, completely blocking out the lights of Atlantic City.

"Thank you," I said weakly.

No acknowledgement.

As his lights disappeared into the darkness ahead of me, I saw not two but three white lights coming towards me. A tugboat towing something far behind it. But word was out about the woman in the sailboat. The tugboat hailed me.

"Two whistles," he said.

Huh? I struggled to remember what that meant.

"I'll pass you on your starboard side."

"Roger that."

He too blotted out the lights of Atlantic City as he passed, and I thought, wow, this really isn't Lake Huron, where we see maybe one ship a night, way off in the distance. I spent the rest of my first night in the ocean in a state of wide-eyed alert.

*May 23*

*Day 2*

*Northeast of Barbuda*

The next morning dawns sunny and warm. The wind is light so we furl in the genoa and raise the spinnaker, a huge, lightweight nylon parachute that makes the most of what wind there is.

Genoa. Spinnaker. It took me a while to learn the names of things. Nothing is straightforward on a boat. The biggest sail, the one that runs up the mast, is the mainsail—that makes sense. But the foresail can have many names. Ours is called a genoa. When I asked Chris why, he looked at me blankly.

"Because the clew extends aft of the mast."

Oh.

We also have a small stormsail that we don't *attach* to the inner forestay, we *hank on*. The inner forestay—and the forestay itself, which the genoa attaches to—is part of the standing rigging, along with the shrouds, the wires that support the mast.

The running rigging is something else altogether, and probably the most complicated system on the boat. To the untrained eye, it looks like an array of ropes attached to various parts of the sails and the boom. But don't call them ropes! You never use the word *rope* on a boat. You call ropes *lines*, and there are specific names for the ones that run up inside the mast and are used to haul the sails up (halyards) and the ones you use to trim the sails—these are called sheets. The mainsail has one sheet and the foresails each have two. So when Chris says release the starboard staysail sheet, I know exactly which rope — sorry, line — I should reach for. And I almost never release the halyard by mistake, which would cause the staysail to come tumbling down.

A gentle swell from behind lifts us slowly, then sets us back down, helping us on our way. Wind-driven waves murmur against the hull. This is not what I thought ocean sailing would be like, and I know it won't always be like this. But for now, it's perfect.

Once we're happy with how the sails are set, I go below and make breakfast. We're having the last two pineapple turnovers from the bakery in English Harbour and coffee — Joy in the Morning, it's called, which seems appropriate. It's a special blend we found at a little place nestled in the hills above Falmouth Harbour. We have a locker full of it, which may be a bit excessive, but the thought of running out of coffee in the middle of the North Atlantic is too grim to contemplate.

We are sprawled comfortably in the cockpit, sipping our coffee. Chris reaches forward and adjusts the sheet so the spinnaker catches a little more wind, then sits back, stretches his arm along the back of the seat. I snuggle in. He smells pretty good for a guy who hasn't showered in a few days. I catch a whiff of his shaving cream. Ocean Breeze, it's called.

"Now you really smell like ocean breeze."

He pulls me close to him, sniffs my hair.

"And you smell like…my girl."

He tucks a strand of hair behind my ear, I smile up at him. Sometimes I think his eyes are brown, but they have flecks of hazel in them, so they change with the light. They are dark brown pools today, uh oh, I know that look.

Our coffee is cold by the time we get back to it. Chris goes below to make another pot.

"Look!" I say, when he returns. In the distance we can see one, then a few, then many dolphins heading towards us. These don't look like ordinary dolphins.

"These are pantropical spotted dolphins," I announce to Chris, who is studying them through his binoculars. I have pulled out the marine mammal guide I keep tucked behind one of the cushions.

"How do you know?"

"Come on, they're easily identified by their white-tipped beak and prominent dark dorsal cape. That light grey swath sweeping upward on their caudal peduncle is distinctive, as is their highly variable degree of spotting."

He lowers his binoculars. I hide the book behind my back.

"Peduncle? Really?"

"You know…that, uh, thing with the grey swath on it."

"Right."

WE MANAGE TO stretch our second pot of coffee to midmorning, by which time Chris, who has been up since 3:00 am, really needs a nap. I decide to try writing a letter to my sister. In theory, we can send email via the single sideband radio, somehow. We haven't tried this out yet. I fetch my computer, make myself comfortable in the cockpit, open it up.

Dear Brenda,

I'm writing to you from the middle of the ocean — well, not the middle, actually. We're somewhere northeast of Antigua, two days out now, maybe another five to go till we make landfall in Bermuda.

I'll bet you didn't expect to hear from me while we were on the crossing. I was a little skeptical when Chris said that we would be able to use the single sideband radio to send email, but it turns out that he was right. It's not that complicated. All you have to do is switch on the radio which is beside the nav station in the salon, then go back to the bedroom and switch the tuner on. Next you connect the modem to the computer, turn on the modem, turn on the computer, and open SailMail on the computer. Then you're ready to tune the antenna. You push the transmit button on the microphone, then run back to the bedroom and adjust the tuner until you get the best signal possible. Back to the nav station, where you log into SailMail on the computer and you're ready to send and receive. Nothing could be simpler.

So far, the sailing has been easy. The winds have been light and steady, the seas calm, the days warm and sunny, and the nights — you would love the nights, Beek. The moon so bright the sails cast a shadow on the water, a stream of sparkling phosphorescence trailing behind us.

This is not at all what I expected. I watched *The Perfect Storm*. Several times. Chris says that's not what it's really like, those are Hollywood waves. Not that he's been across the ocean himself. But he has friends who had to motor all the way from Newfoundland to the Azores, it was so calm. They had to beg diesel fuel from a passing freighter. He also knows some people who endured eight days of gales and heavy seas on their crossing. All they could keep down were crackers and water.

Don't worry, Beek — we have lots of crackers on board, lots of everything, actually. In Antigua, I managed my anxiety about setting out into the ocean by making a complicated provisioning plan and spending several days shopping for groceries, stowing them, checking them, double checking them.

As I was packing and repacking the food lockers, I kept thinking about the day I drove Brad to London. He was so sick by then, you remember what he was like. I knew that this transplant was his one and only chance. If it didn't work — well, I didn't like to think about it.

I got up early that morning, changed the sheets, did a load of wash, put out fresh towels for when we came home. I checked the fridge to make sure there would be milk for our tea. Next thing I knew, I had cleaned out the whole fridge and was walking to the composter with some limp celery, a dried-up orange, half a carton of eggs well past their expiry date.

On my way back to the house, I started picking up apples that had fallen from the tree, throwing them into the composter. Then I spotted a couple of ripe tomatoes in the garden, went to pick them. Look at this mess, I thought, and bent to pull out a few weeds. Half an hour later I straightened up, looked at my watch, it was time to go. I realized that even if I had all the time in the world, I could never be ready enough for what was ahead.

But I don't feel like that now. I think I'm ready. I guess we'll find out.

Who ever really knows what waits ahead, eh, Beek? I never expected to find myself stretched out in the cockpit of a sailboat — my sailboat — water chuckling along the side of the hull, a gentle breeze wafting over me. Right now, the morning sun is shining right through the broad yellow and green stripes of the spinnaker, bathing the cockpit in soft, warm light. I wish you could see this. I hope someday you will.

We're good now, right, Beek? I know you were taken by surprise — shocked, actually, and more than a little angry with me when I announced that I was quitting my job, selling my condo and my car and most of my stuff, and going to sea with a man you'd just met. I didn't introduce him to you sooner, and I'm so sorry about that, but I wanted to be sure. I didn't want anyone to know about Chris, in case it didn't work out.

I did take him to meet Mom, though. Did I ever tell you about that? I knew she would keep my secret, didn't have any choice, actually.

"Oh my god!" she said when I walked into her room at the nursing home with him.

"Hello, Joan," he said awkwardly. She wheeled her chair closer to him, grabbed him with her good hand, you know how strong it is, pulled him close to her, studied his face carefully.

"All right," she said, smiling, releasing his hand. "All right."

She knew, somehow. She was more sure about him, about what we were planning to do, than I was. I'm still not sure I have the courage. For either.

I think you are the brave one in the family, Beek. What you're doing takes a lot more courage than sailing across an ocean. In a couple weeks, I'll be on dry land (with any luck) but you'll still be navigating the shoals of kindergarten, swimming lessons, the tooth fairy. Without any help from Mom, though maybe that's a blessing. She can't tell Anna to watch out! Be careful! Don't touch that! And she can't tell you what you're doing wrong. Not that she'd tell you directly. She'd just purse her lips.

The wind seems to be dying a little. I need to go adjust the sheet, see if I can keep the spinnaker happy, then maybe start thinking about making us some lunch. Chickpea salad again, I think, while we still have red peppers and crunchy carrots. The fresh vegetables aren't going to last long in this heat. Then it will be soup, soup, and more soup. And crackers. Lots of crackers.

I know you're pretty busy, Beek, but do write to me when you can. I can't tell you how many times I've reread your last letter. I can picture Anna in her pink tights and leotard and her soft pink ballet shoes, admiring herself in the mirror. And I can just see her being a butterfly. I'll bet she was good at it!

Congratulations on graduating your first PhD, Beek. That must really feel great. Funny, eh? It doesn't seem that long ago that we were in Montreal, waiting in the hall for the word from your committee. Yet I guess it's more than ten years ago now. And now you're on the committee. Amazing.

You are such a good writer, and I am so grateful for these glimpses into your world. Funny thing—I feel more in touch with you these days, more in tune with what's going on for you, than I felt before we left. Maybe going away for a while is a good thing, in some ways. Makes you see what you left behind a little more clearly.

But not in all ways: I miss your face.

I'd better go. There's a limit to how long an email message can be on SailMail. If you exceed the limit, you will be cut off in mid—

I close the computer with a grin.

AFTER LUNCH, IT's my turn to go down for a serious nap, but it's hard to sleep in the daytime, I just doze, really. From time to time I roll over onto my back, look up through the companionway. The wind ruffles Chris's hair as he scans the horizon for boats. So scruffy. But so handsome. This is how he looked the first time I met him.

I WAS READING the ingredients on the back of a box of muesli when a voice at the end of the aisle cried, "Linda!"

It was Cindy, a woman I used to work with. We had lost touch a few years ago, and now here she was, looking very different than I remembered. She was growing out her hair, and had highlighted it, I think, or else it was sunbleached.

"This is my boyfriend Chris," she said, waving towards the tall, dark-haired man standing behind her. "We've been sailing all summer, just home for a few days," she said breezily. That explained her tanned face and windblown hair.

This guy is trouble, I thought to myself. Too good-looking. Probably full of himself. But there was something about the way he looked me straight in the eye, he was seeing me, really seeing me. It was startling. Suddenly I wished I had changed before coming to the grocery store. My husband Brad and I had stopped in on our way back from our Sunday morning walk in the woods and I was wearing a pair of faded jeans, a work shirt, and my old hiking boots. My hand wandered to my hair. Was the blue jay feather still tucked behind my ear?

But he didn't look much better. Clearly he hadn't showered — his hair looked like he had combed it with his fingers and there was dark stubble on his chin. And his khaki pants and faded black T-shirt had seen many days of wear. I looked down at his feet. Boat shoes. Without socks. My mother had warned me about men who don't wear socks.

But there was something about him. He looked perfectly at ease, not at all self-conscious. This is a man who is comfortable in his own skin, I thought.

"HEY! AM I ever going to get my nap?" Chris calls from the cockpit.

I must have fallen into a sound sleep. I smile up at him, stretch lazily.

"Maybe," I say, pulling the light blanket up to my chin.

He's down the ladder in a flash, tumbles me off the settee.

"Get up, you lazy wench!"

He dives in, closes his eyes, starts snoring softly. Can he really fall asleep that quickly?

"Chris?"

I guess so.

Around mid-afternoon, the wind dies altogether and the spinnaker collapses — no, nothing as sudden as that. It sighs into an exhausted curtain of silky fabric, plasters itself against the rigging, then from time to time rouses itself to flutter around feebly in search of wind before giving up again. I should take it down, but it's a two-person job and I don't want to wake Chris. I try to keep the boat more or less on course, but it's not easy when we're moving so slowly. I look down. The knotmeter reads 0.0. And the chart plotter is blank except for the words *Atlantic Ocean*.

But we're not alone out here — a tropicbird is following us, looking for fish in our wake, perhaps? Uh oh. He has his eye on the pink plastic squid dangling from the fishing line on the stern. I go back and tuck the lure under a coil of rope. (No, don't call it rope.) The tropicbird keeps a close eye on what I'm doing. Hey, that's my squid.

As he hangs in the air above me, I admire his long white tail feather, wonder how on earth he can walk with his feet set so far back on his body. They're practically under his tail. I go below as quietly as I can, grab my bird book.

He can't, it turns out. On land, tropicbirds can move only by pushing themselves forward with their tiny, underdeveloped legs and feet. They spend most of their time at sea, alone or in pairs. Their relationship to other living birds is unclear, the book says. They seem to have no close relatives.

"Are you all alone?" I ask the bird. He doesn't answer.

"Time to motor," Chris says, popping up through the companionway, startling me. Somehow, even asleep, he has sensed that we've stopped moving altogether.

"See my new friend?" I say. But the tropicbird is disappearing in the distance, not interested in us now that the squid seems to be gone.

We go forward and take the spinnaker down, stow it in the V-berth. Then Chris starts the engine and takes the helm while I go down to make supper. It's chicken tonight, poached in coconut milk and lime juice, with a little green curry paste stirred in to make it interesting. I shred some carrots and snow peas to toss into the pan at the last minute. A pot of rice bubbles on the other burner. I'll slice up a ripe mango for dessert.

At 6:30 Chris gathers up the dishes and goes down to listen to Chris Parker's evening forecast.

"Perfect weather for the next few days," he reports, taking off his headphones and switching off the radio. "Winds light and variable, waves less than a metre. So far so good!"

We run through the pre-night checklist—trilight at the top of the mast on, *check*, flashlight in easy reach, *check*, binoculars, *check*. I send Chris down to nap again before he takes the first night watch, then I settle in, feet stretched out in front of me. I watch as the sun dips lower, lower. It passes through a thin band of clouds on the horizon, which glow red, briefly, then fade to pink. The sun flashes between the clouds and the sea, then disappears into the water. I watch as the clouds fade to a soft purple, then darken to grey. I can no longer make out waves in the distance. Then I can't make them out beside the boat. Until the moon rises, we're sailing by the light of the stars, which are surprisingly bright.

I look around the cockpit. This will be my world for the next three weeks. A teak bench long enough for Chris to lie down on curves along the back of the cockpit. It's as beautiful as a piece of fine furniture, each board cut and fitted by hand—Chris's hand, this time. We've had a thick foam cushion custom made for the bench, and we bring pillows up from below, and blankets, when it's cold. It's a comfortable place to nest. Too comfortable sometimes. Staying awake on the night watch can be a challenge.

We're trying a new watch system on this journey. Six-hour night watches are just too long, we discovered on our seven-day passage from the Bahamas to the British Virgin Islands. During the day we will take turns at the helm, adjusting the sails, watching for other ships, keeping an eye on the weather, while the other person naps in the cockpit or reads or does little boat chores. In the afternoon we will each take a long nap, then at 6:00 pm, the night watches will begin. I'll do 6:00 to 9:00 pm, Chris will do 9:00 pm to midnight, I'll do midnight to 3:00 am, and Chris will do 3:00 to 6:00 am.

Along the sides of the cockpit are two narrow teak benches, not so comfortable but a good place to sit when the boat is heeled over—you can wedge your feet against the opposite bench and keep yourself more or less level. They are also a good place to stand.

I put one foot on each of the two side benches, lean on the top of the windshield, which is of course not called a windshield but a spray dodger. From here I have an unobstructed view of the night sky. The breeze ruffles my hair as I watch the stars. I have to remind myself to look around for other ships every now and then, though we still haven't seen another ship since we left Antigua.

But what's that? A pinprick of light the horizon. I jump down from my perch, switch the radar on. Nope. Nothing. But I can see something, and it's getting bigger, which means it's coming closer. I'm reaching for the binoculars when the now-yellowish light resolves itself into a crescent as it rises out of the sea. It's the moon, of course.

IT'S A LOT easier to sleep once it's dark and at 9:00 pm I have to go
below and wake Chris up. Before I go to bed, I make him a thermos
of coffee and hand it up to him along with a little treat.

"Cookies! I didn't know we had cookies," he says, ripping open
the cellophane package.

I've hidden the night watch treats under my T-shirts—if he finds
them, they'll be gone in a week. Or maybe a night.

I sleep soundly and wake at midnight feeling rested and ready
to stand my watch. Chris gives me a quick kiss then dives into the
still-warm berth, pulls the covers up to his chin and starts snoring.
Like most sailors, he can fall asleep instantly. He also wakes at the
slightest sound—I try not to adjust the sails while he's asleep or
he leaps out of bed fully alert and ready to deal with whatever is
going on.

I step up onto the side benches again, lean on the dodger. The
moon has risen but the stars are as bright as before. Brighter, even. I
scan for boats. Nothing.

So much room out here. So much time to think.


I TOOK POSSESSION of the condo on the first of January—was it
really just four years ago? It feels like a lifetime. I picked up the keys
from the real estate developer's office, but it was another week before
I could bring myself to go there. This is silly, I told myself. You'll be
moving in at the end of the month.

I had bought a unit in an old school in downtown Waterloo that
was being converted into condos. Cindy and Chris lived there, so at
least there would be someone I knew in the building. I was nervous
about living alone

I made myself stop in on the way home from work. With a heavy
heart, I turned the key in the lock, fumbled for the light switch. The
door clicked softly shut behind me and there I stood in my long
black coat and winter boots, alone in my condo for the first time.
The heat was off—I could see my breath. Rush hour traffic was
lined up on the street outside my window, exhaust rising in the still
night air. The light changed. A delivery truck honked impatiently.

Traffic began to move. Home, I thought. They're all going home. For dinner.

I made myself look around the condo. The workers had finished moving the wall, converting what had been the library of the old school into a one-bedroom unit rather than two. I wanted there to be room for the dining room table from the farm, and anyway, what did I need a second bedroom for? The painters had almost finished. Was green the right colour after all? Was it too dark? I'd never chosen paint colours on my own before.

*Look at you. You can't even pick a paint colour.*

I made myself walk into the little galley kitchen, stood in front of the sink, leaned on the granite counter. Cooking for one. After all these years. How would I do it? I walked quickly to the door, switched off the light, locked the door behind me.

I CLIMB DOWN from my perch, check our course and speed, look at the oil and temperature gauges, scan the horizon for ships — nothing. I curl up on the bench, gaze out at the ribbon of moonlight on the water behind us.

IT WAS SNOWING heavily the day I moved in. Where do you want this? the movers would ask. Just put it there, I would say, waving my hand vaguely. I wanted it to be over, wanted them out of there, wanted nothing more than to be alone.

And then I was.

I scooped up Emily, lay down on the couch, and hugged my little bulldog. She squirmed to be let down, but I held her tightly, looked up at the strange new ceiling, listened to the sound of traffic outside my window. They're all going home.

The next morning my sister Brenda called to check in on me.

"How's the unpacking going?" she asked.

"Um, not very well, actually. I can't decide where to put things. I was wondering, could you come over and help me?"

"Of course. I have to take Anna for her three-month check-up this morning, but that shouldn't take long."

It was two o'clock before Brenda appeared at my door. She handed me the baby, stamped the snow from her boots, shrugged out of her L.L. Bean parka.

"Sorry I'm so late. It's snowing like crazy," she said, pulling off her toque and running her fingers through her dark hair, so much shorter now. "The drive took forever. Okay, where do we start?"

"My books," I said, pointing to a huge pile of boxes in the corner.

"How do you want them?"

"It doesn't matter," I said.

"Right," she said, trying to hide her concern. She knew I'd spent money I didn't have on custom-built floor-to ceiling bookshelves. No more storing my books in boxes in the basement.

"Let's just put them on the shelves for now. You can rearrange them later."

As we unpacked box after box, I came across books I'd forgotten I had. My tiny perfect Edward Gorey books. I flipped open my favourite, *The Gashlycrumb Tinies*.

*A* is for Amy who fell down the stairs.

*B* is for Basil assaulted by bears.

All these hapless children meeting untimely deaths. I flipped to Neville, who died of ennui. There he was, staring out the window, the top of his tiny head just peeking over the sill.

We worked until the light began to fade, Anna sleeping happily in the little nest of pillows we'd made for her on the couch, Emily snuggled up beside her, snoring as only a bulldog can. I'm not sure which one was sweeter, Anna in her soft pink sleeper or Emily. I sat down beside my little dog, stroked her smooth tawny-brown coat, her bat-like ears which perked straight up, even as she slept, her wrinkled face, her black button of a nose.

"I've got to go," Brenda said. She woke Anna gently and began zipping her into her snowsuit. "What are you having for supper?"

"I've got something in the fridge," I said.

She knew I was lying. She rummaged in her bag. "Here," she said, handing me a plastic freezer container. "It's eggplant and noodles. Just throw it in the oven for half an hour."

"Thanks, Beek."

Don't go, I wanted to say to her. Please stay. I need you. Her daughter needed her more, I understood that. But it didn't make it any easier to see her go.

She hesitated at the door, gave me a big hug, then held me at arm's length, squeezed my shoulders tightly.

"You'll be all right, you know. Just give it time."

*P* is for Prue trampled flat in a brawl. She didn't see it coming. How could she? Her mother has sent her to fetch her father home from the bar. She's just being a good little girl. She reaches for the door handle, has to stand on her tiptoes, she's so tiny. And then.

A SCHOOL OF flying fish bursts out of the water off our port bow, trying to avoid us, perhaps, or maybe pursued by something under water. Or perhaps they're just flying for the sheer joy of it. I often have to pick them off the deck in the morning, tiny creatures, maybe five inches long, with big dark eyes that give them a look of perpetual surprise. Am I supposed to be flying? Or maybe, what's this boat doing out here?

*What are you doing out here? You're afraid of everything.*

*May 24*

~~~~~~

*Day 3*

"You're quiet this morning."

It's another perfect day. The winds have picked up a little and we've put the genoa back out, switched the engine off. We're sailing again.

"Just thinking," I say, forcing a smile.

"About what?" he asks, refilling my coffee mug, topping up his.

"Do you really want to know?"

"Yes." He's a brave man.

So I tell him. It's May 24th. Today would have been my thirtieth wedding anniversary.

"Why is it still so hard for me?"

*Because you can't let go. You're pathetic.*

"These things take time," Chris says.

He puts his cup down, reaches for the winch handle, tightens the sheet slightly so the genoa catches a little more of the light winds. I watch it belly out with each gentle gust, then slacken. The sun is warm on my face.

I HAD BEEN dreading my first wedding anniversary alone, almost made it through the day, but around three o'clock I left the office in tears, came home, made myself a big mug of tea, took it to bed. Emily followed me into the bedroom. We're napping now? Okay. She hopped up on the bed, curled up at my feet and was asleep in no time. I sat with the quilt up over my knees, watched the curtains breathe in and out in the warm spring breeze. Breathe in and out, in and out. That's all you have to do.

I put my empty mug on the dresser, curled up under the quilt, napped a little, I think, but mostly I just watched the sun move across the room, looked at the pattern the lace curtains made, on the quilt, on the rug, on the wall. I could smell roses outside the window. At the farm at this time of year, it would have been lilacs.

Emily snored all afternoon, then around five o'clock, decided she'd had enough. She hopped down off the bed, sat in the hall outside the door looking at me. You coming?

"Okay," I said. "You're right. Enough."

The narrow yard at the back of the condo had been turned into a formal flower garden. It was one of the things I liked about the place. While Emily sniffed around, I could stroll up and down the path and look at flowers that someone else took care of. But that day the sight of the peonies starting to bud, the iris just coming into bloom was too much for me.

Chris found me sitting on the back step, hugging my knees, my eyes red from crying. He put his recycling in the bin, then sat down beside me.

"What's up?"

I hadn't seen him around much that spring. Cindy was off travelling and he'd been spending most of his time at the boat. I didn't really know him very well, but there was something about the way he just sat there, waiting patiently, that made it all come pouring out. I told him that twenty-six years ago, I'd married the boy from the farm across the road. I was nineteen.

"I didn't know anything about farming," I said. "We were just renters, Dad worked in town. Fortunately, an elderly aunt came with his grandmother's farm. She did her best to teach me how to be a farm wife, always wash the clothes on Monday, have them out on the line by nine in the morning or the neighbours will think you're a slattern. I had to look that up — slattern.

"'Plant a big garden,' she would say. 'Raise some chickens, keep the freezer full. Make pies on Saturday in case somebody drops by after church. Have a house without a pie,' she would say, 'be ashamed until you die.'"

"I would have to agree with that," Chris said.

"It took me a while, but I started to get the hang of it, was happy, even."

Emily had given up sniffing the flower beds and was snoring at my feet. I leaned over and stroked her soft ears.

"That's one ugly dog," he said.

"No, she's beautiful! Look at her little turned-up nose."

"Looks like she ran into a wall."

I pulled her up onto my lap, hugged her tightly. She grumbled a little, but was snoring again in no time.

"I never expected to be living in town, alone. I don't want this."

We sat in silence for a while. He was watching the sky, the sun was setting, the clouds fading to purple. I was watching him, so at ease with himself, leaning against the red-brick wall of the old school, long legs stretched out in front of him.

"So what's the hardest thing for you right now?" he asked.

"Grocery shopping."

"Come on," he said, standing up and brushing off his jeans, tucking in his T-shirt.

"I can't," I said. "Not looking like this."

"Yes, you can. Go get your wallet."

At work the next day, a colleague said she had seen me coming out of the grocery store with a man.

"He was dreamy. Who was that?"

"Just a friend."


"THIS DAY WON'T always be so hard for you, I promise," Chris says, tucking a wayward strand of hair behind my ear.

I smile at him. This morning his eyes are more hazel than brown.

"What day?" I say.


THE WINDS ARE still light, but we're holding three knots, which is good enough for us. We've decided that if we drop below three knots, we'll motor, though we're keenly aware that we can't motor all the way across the ocean—we don't have enough fuel, even with both tanks full and all the extra jerrycans. So we're sailing gently along, nothing much to do but watch the sky, look around for other boats every now and then.

I've been keeping an eye on a cloud that's appeared on the horizon, off to the east. It's darker than the white fluffy clouds we've been seeing, and lower. And it seems to be growing.

"I don't like the looks of that," I say, pointing to what is slowly turning into a bank of dark clouds.

"Me either. Looks like a squall. And it's coming towards us."

"Reduce sail?"

"No, I think we can sail around it. Let's tack."

We've been sailing northeast. If we tack, we'll be heading northwest. We're not moving very fast, but if we change course, maybe the squall will pass behind us.

As luck would have it, the wind picks up just as the squall approaches and we pick up speed. Four knots, five, six. All we get is a few splatters of rain as the edge of the squall passes over us.

"That was fun," Chris says, as the boat starts to slow again. Five, four, three. The squall is heading off towards the horizon. We're back in full sun again, but it's much cooler now, nice.

"I'm going down for my nap," Chris says. "Do you want your book?"

"Sure. Thanks."

But I don't really feel like reading. I hold the book in my lap, watch the sky.

WE WERE JUST kids, really. We didn't tell anyone, just had the minister in the village marry us. The minister's wife served us white cake and ginger ale at the manse afterwards. There was a lace cloth on the table, a big vase of roses on the heavy wooden sideboard. The house smelled of lemon wax.

Then we went and told our parents what we had done.

Brad's father was working in the yard.

"Hey, Dad," Brad began.

"Where have you been? You were supposed to help me..."

He turned around, saw me in a long, unbleached cotton dress, a little lace at the throat, Brad in his best brown corduroy pants and plaid shirt.

"We got married, Dad."

They'd hoped for more for their only son, a girl from a good farm family, someone from their church, at least. I was glad I didn't have to face his mother—she was in town shopping for the day. His father gave us his credit card so we could go out for a nice dinner.

My mother insisted that we come back home afterwards, and to my horror, there were cars lined up the laneway, people milling around the lawn, if you could call it that, eyeing the overgrown flower beds. The house had a crumbling cement porch on the side of it, the wooden roof and railing long gone, really just a set of precarious steps going up to the kitchen door. We never used the front door.

"Surprise," Mom sang, as she emerged from the house carrying a slab cake she must have found at the store in Plattsville. The tiny bride and groom that had decorated her wedding cake stood forlornly in an expanse of almost-white icing.

My husband's grandmother inspected the cake closely before accepting a piece. She locked eyes with his mother. See what kind of family your son has married into?

"Tea? Coffee?" Mom was handing around mismatched cups. Some had saucers, some didn't.

ENOUGH OF THIS. Enough. I scan the horizon, no boats in sight, open my book.

We're reading our way through Patrick O'Brian's novels about the adventures of Jack Aubrey, an officer in the British Royal Navy, and his ship's surgeon, Stephen Maturin, set during the Napoleonic Wars. It's a struggle to keep ahead of Chris, who reads on his night watch rather than gazing at the stars.

When we were in Antigua, I found myself looking around English Harbour, wondering how much it had changed since Jack and Stephen were stationed there, had to keep reminding myself that Jack and Stephen aren't real. Chris likes Jack, the man of action, but I identify with quiet, introverted Stephen, who knows nothing about sailing and spends his time studying birds.

Stephen doesn't have to sail the boat—his job is patching sailors together after battles with other ships, sawing off arms and legs as necessary, a messy business. But I am the first mate on this ship—the only mate, actually, though I prefer to call myself the cabin boy because I am responsible for keeping things in good order below, taking care of the cooking and cleaning and just generally looking after our creature comforts. Chris had to teach me how to use a winch—always wind the sheet on in a clockwise direction, keep your hair tied back so it doesn't get caught, harder, crank harder. I watched him set and trim the sails until I more or less got the hang of it, learned how to scan for boats properly—you don't just look around haphazardly—how to check our course and speed, how to use the radar. We spent two summers sailing the Great Lakes while I learned how to sail. But there are still times when I feel like Stephen.

Oh, yeah. Stephen isn't real.

CHRIS DOESN'T NAP for long—it's too nice a day to spend below.

"I'm going to do a little fishing," Chris says, rummaging in his tackle box. He pulls out spoon boy, his lucky lure, attaches it to a length of wire, ties it onto his fishing line. He goes to the back deck and drops the lure into the water, lets out some line, then props the rod in the holder screwed to the back deck. He stands, one hand curled around the backstay, and watches the lure spinning through the deep blue water. He's still in his underwear. Life just doesn't get much better than this.

I'm starting to think about what to make for dinner when Chris yells, "Fish on!"

I look back just in time to see a silvery-blue flash as a big fish leaps out of the water, then plunges back in, shaking its head from side to side.

"Heave to!" Chris says.

I can handle that in these light winds. I turn the boat up into the wind until the genoa backwinds, stopping us dead.

"Get the net! No, the gaff! Get the net and the gaff!"

I scramble to the back deck, untie the net and gaff from the radar arch. He's managed to get the fish up to the stern of the boat, but it's still got a lot of fight left in it.

"The gaff!"

I hand him a long pole with a hook on the end, sharpened to a nasty point. I can't watch.

"Sorry, buddy," I hear Chris murmur. Then I hear it flopping around on the back deck.

"Wow! What is it? It looks like a tuna."

"I think it might be. Ten pounds at least. Get the rum."

I hurry below deck, come back with a bottle of cheap rum. I watch as he pours some into the fish's gills.

"There you go, buddy," Chris says.

"I'll go get your filleting knife."

When I come back, the fish is lying there in a drunken stupor. Or dead. I'm not sure which. Chris may have knocked him on the head while I was below. I've brought our guide to ocean fish so we can identify him before Chris gets to work. We study its shape, its colour, the placement of its fins. It's a slender, streamlined fish, slightly flat, its back a beautiful iridescent bluish green, silvery sides. It's a King Mackerel, we decide, a member of the tuna family. Definitely something we can eat.

Half an hour later he hands me a big bowl full of fillets. I try not to look at the back deck, but of course I do. It's slick with blood. I duck back down into the galley. We'll have King Mackerel steaks tonight, poached mackerel tomorrow, mackerel with rice and peas the next day. Then what? There's no room in the freezer yet.

Jim would know what to do with all this fish.

WE WERE AT anchor in Staniel Cay in the Bahamas. The front had passed over us and the winds had dropped and settled in from the north—good winds for setting out for Antigua. The seas were still running high, though, so we decided to spend one more day in the Bahamas and head out the next morning.

The call came over the radio just as we were finishing our coffee.

"*MonArk, MonArk—Salty Paws.*"

"*Salty Paws—MonArk.* Go seven-one."

"Seven-one."

Chris punched in 7–1 and said, "Good morning, Jim."

"Good morning, Chris. We're going hunting this morning and wondered if you'd like to join us."

Chris looked at me doubtfully. We'd just drawn up a list of things we had to do before we set out.

"Go," I said. "We can change the oil and check the batteries in the morning."

"Sure," Chris said eagerly. "What time?"

"We'll be there in five minutes."

There was a flurry of flippers and mask and wetsuit and don't forget to sunblock your nose, then he was down the ladder and racing off across the bay with Jim and Bentley. Three boys in a rubber dinghy with spears. I wasn't sorry to be left behind.

I really don't get this hunting thing. I like fresh fish as much as the next person—I just have trouble looking at a beautiful reef fish gently nibbling at the coral, then seeing it thrashing on the end of a spear. I go along with Chris when it's just the two of us—it isn't safe to hunt alone. The current through the cuts between the ocean and the bank can be fierce, and you have to keep an eye out for sharks, especially if you're lucky enough to spear something. Sharks can smell blood a mile away. So I follow him in the dinghy, not so close that I spook the fish, but close enough that he can get his catch—and himself—out of the water quickly, if necessary.

But not that morning. I was off the hook, so to speak. I looked at the list. I was planning to make muffins, wash my hair. Instead I poured myself another cup of coffee and reached for my book.

A couple of hours later, I heard a dinghy zooming across the bay and looked up. Jim cut the engine and Chris grabbed the swim ladder at the stern. They were all smiles.

"I speared a huge queen triggerfish," Chris said, "and Bentley got a lobster."

Lobsters are pretty scarce now, so this was big news. Bentley held it up for me to admire. It was a big one. Chris eyed it hungrily.

"Why don't you guys come over for dinner?" Chris suggested. "Between the triggerfish and the lobster, there's enough to feed us all. Say around 5:30?"

Dinner for four. In about three hours. Yikes. The mail boat had come in since we provisioned for the journey. Maybe we could find some fresh produce.

There are two grocery stores in Staniel Cay—the pink one and the blue one. They're just a couple of doors apart, so you pretty much have to visit both of them if you don't want to hurt anyone's feelings. We started at the pink store, at the top of the hill.

The pink store is in a building about the size of a two-car garage. For some reason, there are no lights inside, and no windows, either. What little light there is comes in through the open door. You have to wait until your eyes adjust to the darkness before you can start shopping.

Just inside the door there was a table piled high with potatoes—local, by the look of it, with dirt still clinging to them. Beneath the table was a big bag of onions.

"Look at this," Chris said. The bag was stamped "Chatham, Ontario." Chris grew up in Chatham.

We picked out a couple onions and half a dozen potatoes, looked around in vain for any other produce. Nope. While Chris wandered up and down the aisles—all three of them—I rummaged through the freezer at the back of the store, a chest freezer, the kind people have in their basements. A couple of skinned knuckles later, I came up with a not-too-freezer-burned chicken. We presented our purchases to the woman behind the counter, who looked them—and us—over carefully, then slid a calculator towards us. We hadn't seen her punch anything in. It read $17.40. I guess we were standard $17.40-looking boaters. While I paid her, Chris loaded our purchases into his backpack.

Though the blue store is much more promising-looking, it had even less to offer. There were screens on the doors, and bright light streamed through the windows — windows! Three of them. The floor was covered with linoleum and the items offered for sale were arranged neatly on shelves lining the walls — cans of icing, toothpaste, small bottles of dishwashing liquid, canned beans. I checked the fridge — they had milk and eggs, both of which we can always use more of. We looked hopefully around for fresh produce. A couple of weather-beaten green peppers and some pale, hard tomatoes, the kind we get in Canada in the winter. Some too-green bananas. Pyramids of potatoes and onions. That was it.

As we hurried back to the boat, I said to Chris, "At least we have lots of eggs now. I can make fresh pasta. That should fill them up. And we can serve rum drinks with lots of lime juice so no one dies of scurvy."

Back at the boat, Chris tidied up while I made the pasta dough. I was almost done running the last strip through the pasta machine when our guests arrived. Jim handed me a covered dish — he was going to do something with the lobster. I slipped it into the oven without looking at it, put a pot of water on to boil for the pasta, then tried to figure out what to do with the triggerfish. Something simple. I melted a glob of butter in the big frying pan, chopped some garlic and swished it around, then gently simmered the fish. Lemon pepper — that's what it needed. I sprinkled generously.

Fresh pasta takes no time to cook, and dinner was ready in about ten minutes. I put a big bowl of pasta, a small plate of triggerfish in garlic butter, and Jim's dish on the table. Chris opened the bottle of crisp white wine Jim and Bentley had brought and Jim removed the lid from his dish. I couldn't believe my eyes. It was lobster thermidor, juicy chunks of steamed lobster swimming in a heavy cream-sherry sauce, fresh parmesan melted on top, garnished with a sprig of fresh rosemary. Fresh rosemary? Clearly Jim was much better at provisioning than I am.

And making the most of what the ocean offers.

THE WIND DROPS at sunset, as it often does. We're creeping along in the soft darkness, holding three knots at best, but we've decided that's good enough. It's hard to sleep with the engine thrumming. We opt for a quiet night.

Too quiet, maybe. The story I haven't let myself think much about has started running through my mind. I seem to have no choice but to follow it.

WE HAD MOVED into a tiny apartment in town, were both working at jobs in the city when Brad's grandfather died. He decided that he wanted to buy the family farm from his grandmother. What? I had no idea he wanted to farm.

"Okay," I said, "but I'm going to university in the fall." I'd already picked my courses.

The man from Farm Credit was stern with me.

"You'll quit school and work if you have to."

"Sure," I said.

No way, I thought.

We both kept working full-time through the spring and summer. Evenings we'd go over plans for the new barn, make little changes—an extra fan here, a sliding door there, maybe another bank of lights above the breeding pens. It was exhausting, but even I was starting to get excited about this new venture. A hundred sows, we were going to run, farrow to finish. Finally Farm Credit gave us the go-ahead and we started to build.

I started school that September, continued working part-time off the farm, helped in the barn in the evenings. Which didn't leave much time for studying. I would wait until Brad fell asleep at night then get up quietly and read into the early hours. English literature. What are you going to do with that? my mother-in-law would say. She took to telling people that I was studying journalism. At least that was something useful.

We decided to get a few sheep, make use of our front pasture, which wasn't good for much else. The neighbours thought we were crazy—there's no money in sheep. They watched closely as we divided the front pasture into narrow strips. It was a lot of work. We'd load the sledgehammer, steel rails, and wire into the wheelbarrow and work our way slowly down to the road and back. I think it took us almost a month altogether, squeezing the fencing in on weekends, but it worked, it kept the sheep from grazing the pasture to the ground.

We had no equipment, so we rented the land out to a cashcropper. Between that income and my job and the pigs and the sheep, it looked like it was going to work. And it did. For a while.

I WATCH THE stars for a bit, look around halfheartedly—I'd be surprised to see another boat out here. Maybe I should read my book. But I've been reading all afternoon. I'm all read out.

Stephen and Jack don't have to stand night watches. They have crew to do that. The two of them spend their evenings in Jack's cabin, making music—Jack plays the violin, Stephen the cello—and eating toasted cheese.

I check our course and speed, look at the gauges.

Mmm. I could do with some toasted cheese right now. Where's my steward?

I decide to check my email, creep below deck and log onto SailMail. To my great surprise and delight, Brenda has written back already. I do a quick look around, then settle in to read her message.

Dear Linda,

Isn't it all so strange? You are far out in the Atlantic (or not so far, if the winds have remained light) and I am at work on holiday Monday (not so strange, actually.) But that's fine because it's raining and cool and everything I planted yesterday will be loving the rain. I am here trying to get my head around a semi-structured anxiety disorders interview schedule that I have to teach on Wednesday, and you are probably trying to get your head around the idea that you are out in the ocean, heading towards Bermuda and who-knows-where next.

I'm sure you didn't mean to be funny, but your last letter made me laugh out loud. How can you doubt that you have the courage to sail across an ocean? You're out there, aren't you? That's more than most people would be brave enough to do. And besides, at this point, what choice do you have? You will handle the challenges, I'm sure of it, and feel very proud of yourself when you reach the other side.

Finding the courage to be in a relationship again after all you've been through is the greater challenge, I would think. I remember you writing to me from the Dismal Swamp one evening to tell me that you had a miserable cold and Chris was in the galley cooking dinner, because you didn't really feel like eating, never mind cooking. It astonished you. You were not used to being taken care of. His tenderness moved you to tears. Which is kind of sad, in a way. How did you get to such a ripe old age without knowing what it's like to be looked after?

You're already well on your way, my dear. Intimacy is something that builds over time, in the small moments. You can do it. You are doing it.

But enough of this. I hope you're not rolling your eyes and saying if this is what passes for sisterly advice, thank god she's 2,000 miles away.

I think I told you that Chuck and I are going on vacation for a week? Without Anna? This will be the first time we've left her for more than a few days, and I am having horribly anxious moments at night while in bed, about leaving her. Nothing logical (I know: separations are good; she and Peggy are a good match; all is arranged for her dance class, daycare trips, etc; a trip is important for Chuck and me; Anna handles separations well, she's had practice, although we've never been away from her before for more than one or two days.)

Nope, nothing logical. Just a terrific aching in my heart, as though something is being ripped out. I feel as though I am abandoning the most fragile, precious thing I ever had to care for. I can see her face looking anxiously out the window, watching me as I go.

I feel acutely aware of the imbalance in our relationship with her, in that, while we understand that planes fly both ways, that there are logical physical connections between places in he world, and that if we needed to we could fly right back to her, she does not. She could not go to the airport and find us, if need be; she could not seek us out. Hell, she couldn't even call us on the phone independently. Not that she would ever need to.

But imagine knowing—being acutely aware—that you cannot do any of these things, and that the people you need most in the world are voluntarily leaving you, without recourse, "for a little vacation." It feels terrible.

She has been preparing in her way—making little ziplock bags of things for us to take (several pennies and a bus token; handmade cards with her name written all over them; a little travel soap; some pictures of her and us; two unmatched doll socks). She seems to be both protecting and preparing us, and afraid that we will forget her. It is breaking my heart. She is desperately trying to map out what this separation will be, in four-year-old-time. And she looks so serious, so afraid, and so angry when the numbers slowly go by: four, five six…

So how am I going to survive the vacation? Chuck says that wine and sun and a sandy beach will help, but I am a bit afraid. I am also a little afraid that I have let her take too big a space in my life. Does this mean I am too involved with her? Am I having an identity crisis at the thought of being away from her? Aren't those things terrible pathological mothering errors? Or is it normal mother-of-a-preschooler stuff?

So it's a weird twist, eh, that I am equally worried for her and me. Maybe I need a transitional object, a blankie, a soother… Sheesh. Or sixteen more years of therapy.

When you told me you were running away to sea, I wasn't really angry, Linda. I was afraid, I think. Not *for* you, so much, but of losing you. I was settling into a life I really wanted, my home and husband, career, and now my new baby. But it was a huge step for me and one I had hoped to take with you. Then you changed.

In what seemed like a heartbeat you went from a sad, devastated middle-aged woman into something unfamiliar. Suddenly you were doing things you had never done before ("I'm off sailing with a friend for the weekend."). Sailing? Friend? Instead of sitting alone in your condo, you started hiking in the woods for hours, by yourself, driving to Toronto—on the 401! And you began to look different. Have I ever told you that I once drove past you on King Street in Waterloo, looked right at you, but did not realize until a few blocks later that it was you? Short skirt, flirty blouse, long hair. Who was that?

You grew and flourished, and I panicked. I was losing the person who helped shape my life, who helped me understand things, the woman who showed up at my house one rainy day with a pair of new rubber boots for me, insisting we go to the conservation area to walk in the flooded creek. I loved that part of me, the part I was with you. Like the twin in *The Orchid Hunter*, who was so close to his brother that he never really had an experience until he had the chance to talk to his brother about it. The telling of it made it true. That was us. And then it wasn't.

And I can't say that I am proud of how I responded, with anger and accusations of irresponsibility and irrationality. How could you think of doing something so foolhardy with someone who, to my mind, was too handsome, too confident, and too flighty? How could you?

Now, a year later, I see that I was afraid of losing you, but I also recognize my fear of growing older and smaller in the world I was about to enter, while you grew younger and freer.

So a sad mix of jealousy and fear made me angry and unable to see how happy you were. I did not believe it. I think sometimes that it took me forever to really get that you were going (I am, in so many ways, painfully like a four-year-old), and now I alternate between great excitement for you and acute longing to cling to your leg and whine (see?).

But so far, it's been fine. In fact, these letters make me feel closer to you than ever. I feel sure now that we can do more than just wave at each other across the distance.

Must go now. It's time to take Anna to her riding lesson. Yes, we've given up on swimming and taken up horseback riding—both of us! See? You're not the only one having adventures.

Love you,
Beek

## May 25

~~~~~

## Day 4

Our fourth day out and so far we've managed to make 100 miles a day, even in these light winds. We've both been secretly hoping for more, but 100 miles a day isn't bad — it will get us to Bermuda in ten days.

In the meantime, it's sunny and warm, just a few fluffy clouds on the horizon. There's a ten- to fifteen-knot wind from the east and we're sailing steadily north, right where we want to go, on a comfortable beam reach. The seas are calm, the wind-driven waves less than a foot, backed by a gentle three- to four-foot swell. It's all good.

Almost all. Just after lunch, I look up from my book and see something up ahead in the distance. The clouds on the horizon are bunching together and piling up — they're still fluffy on top, but they're flat on the bottom and getting darker. But that's not what's troubling me. It's very faint, but it's definitely there: a funnel rising from the surface of the water into the clouds. It doesn't seem to be moving as a tornado would, it's just sitting in one spot. But we're sailing right towards it.

"Chris?" I say. "Better come have a look at this."

"A waterspout," he says calmly. Too calmly. Clearly this isn't good.

"Get ready to tack," he says.

He turns the boat into the wind, then across the wind. The genoa starts to backwind and I release the port sheet, pull the genoa in on the starboard side. The main tacks by itself. Chris keeps turning until we're sailing steadily south, away from the waterspout. We both look back. It has already started to dissipate, and a minute later it's gone. Cautiously, we tack again and resume our previous course.

"That was a bit surreal," I say.

"Yeah," says Chris. "I've never seen one that close."

"Are we in for some bad weather?"

"Not necessarily. That was a fair-weather waterspout—I've seen them on the Great Lakes. The really dangerous ones form in thunderstorms, behave more like a tornado."

I don't much like the sound of that.

"I'll take the helm for a while," he says casually. "Why don't you go down for a nap?"

But I can't fall asleep. I try to think of the worst weather we've encountered so far. Surprisingly, it wasn't in the ocean: it was in the Great Lakes.

WE WERE AT anchor one hot, sunny afternoon, in Lake Erie, just off Pelee Island. I was up in the cockpit, trimming my nails, when the sky suddenly clouded over, then turned a menacing shade of purple, then black.

"Chris?"

He came up from below, wiping his oily hands on a rag. We could see lightning coming our way, could hear the rumble of thunder, growing louder.

"Shouldn't we go to shore?" I asked him.

"We won't have that option in the ocean. Let's pull anchor and see if we can get around Lighthouse Point before it hits."

We didn't quite make it. A wall of wind heeled us over just as we were rounding the point. Eight knots. Nine. It took all of Chris's strength to keep the boat from turning up into the wind, which would have put us on the rocks. I ran forward to pull in the genoa, but I wasn't able to: the furling gear had jammed. There was nothing to do but let the sheet go and spill the wind from the sail.

"Get back in here!" Chris shouted from the cockpit.

I was already on my way. The genoa was flailing around in the wind, could easily have knocked me overboard. Or out.

Suddenly we were in the lee of the point and I was able to take the wheel while Chris dealt with the furling gear.

The thunderstorm itself was nothing compared to the blast of wind that came before it. But I think both of us were shaken. Well, I was, at least. And even Chris was a little pale. He told me later that when we hit eleven knots, the bow started to dig in, something that had never happened before. Letting the sheet go was the right thing to do—we needed to slow the boat down, and fast.

We learned a few things that day: Never take your eye off the sky, even on a clear, sunny day. Reduce sail as soon as you see a weather system approaching.

And furling gear will always jam just when you need it the most.

*May 26*

~~~~~~

*Day 5*

It's mackerel with rice and peas tonight, a high-end version of boat gorp—rice cooked in canned mushroom soup with a tin of tuna and a can of peas thrown in.

From time to time, I look up from the simmering pot—I'm waiting till the rice is almost cooked to add the mackerel and peas. Outside the galley window, the sea is the most incredible shade of blue; I never get tired of looking at it. Sun sparkles on the water as far as the eye can see. We're sailing in a sea of diamonds. I cut the mackerel into chunks, stir it into the rice, dump in the can of peas. When I look out again, a band of puffy white clouds has formed on the horizon.

By the time I emerge from below with two steaming bowls of gorp, they've turned into a band of dark clouds.

"I don't think it's going to rain," Chris says. He digs in. "Mmm. This is great."

As we eat our dinner, he checks our position. Another 100-mile day despite the light winds. So far so good. But the dark clouds are getting closer. They're also getting darker.

They're almost on us by the time we finish eating.

"Maybe we'd better tie in a couple of reefs," he says, handing me his empty bowl. "Why don't you go below and close up."

When I get back, Chris has already shortened sail and zipped up the canvas around the cockpit.

"Maybe it *is* going to rain," he says. Big drops of rain are splattering on the windscreen and there's lightning in the distance.

Not the pretty kind that dances around the tops of the clouds. Big, angry bolts of lightning are stabbing the water. And they're getting closer.

We've never been struck by lightning, and may we never be, though they say that sooner or later, every voyaging sailboat gets hit. In theory, steel boats are rarely damaged by a lightning strike, and injuries or deaths by lightning are uncommon. With so much steel in contact with the water, the electrical charge just dissipates harmlessly into the surrounding water. In theory. But I check the abandon-ship kit just in case, make sure it's zipped up, ready to go, in easy reach. My bigger fear is that we'll get hit and Chris will be knocked unconscious—or worse. For the first time, I feel a long way from shore.

The wall of clouds is on us now, rain pelting, thunder crashing, lightning all around.

"Don't touch the steel," I remind Chris.

"You either."

The wind heels us over, even with the tiny bit of sail we have up, burying the port rail in the water. Six knots, seven, seven and a half. Suddenly it begins to ease up.

"There," Chris says. "I think that was the worst of it." He switches on the radar to confirm that the bank of clouds is moving away, spends a little too long looking at the screen, zooms out, then out further.

"What's wrong?"

"This squall is moving off, but there's another one right behind it, and behind it, there's something so big and black I can't see the other side of it."

I do the only sensible thing: I go below and put the spare GPS and the handheld radio in the oven, which is somehow isolated from the rest of the boat. That way, if we're struck by lightning and all our electronics are knocked out, we'll at least be able to tell where we are and call for help.

Bless this woman, I think.

I'D PUT IT off as long as I could: it was time to do the wash. The sheets were grubby, the towels stiff with salt, and I was wearing Chris's clothes because everything I owned was dirty. (All he ever wore in the Bahamas was his bathing suit, which got "clean" every time he went for a swim.) Our clothes weren't "I think I may have worn this once" dirty—they were mustard-smear, lubricating-oil, sweat-stain, coffee-dribble dirty.

Finding a place to do the wash in a string of islands with no fresh water was a bit of a challenge. Fortunately, we weren't far from Black Point Settlement, a small town that seems to have figured out how to desalinate ocean water on a large scale. There was free fresh water available at the town tap—all you had to do was bring a wrench to turn the tap on and off—and wonder of wonders, there was a laundromat in town.

We were anchored at Staniel Cay, about five miles from Black Point, tucked in between two islands in a protected little spot. There was a front coming through that night, with strong winds that would clock around from the southwest to the northeast. We were pretty sure that if we pulled anchor and sailed to Black Point to do the wash, our spot would be gone when we returned. So we decided to dinghy there.

The seas were calm, the afternoon sunny and warm—no sign of the bad weather to come. We packed our clothes into plastic bags, loaded them into the dinghy, and headed out. The plan was that Chris would leave me in Black Point and return to Staniel to fill the diesel tanks, which involved lugging jerrycans of fuel from shore. I was pretty sure I had the better deal.

Chris helped me haul our stuff from the public dock to the laundromat, a distance of about three city blocks, a unit of measurement that would make no sense to the people of Black Point. There's just one main road, running along the coast. There weren't many boats in the harbour that day. Black Point is completely exposed to anything but an east wind, so the usually busy anchorage was empty except for a handful of local fishing boats that looked like they could weather just about anything—and probably had.

Chris helped me sort our clothes into washers—five of them—and pumped in quarters while I poured in the soap. Then I walked him back to the dock. Once he'd disappeared around the point, I turned and walked back through the town, feeling a little conspicuous. School had let out, and kids were straggling down the road in little groups, talking excitedly and calling to one another.

They greeted me politely as they passed, suddenly on their best behaviour. "Hello," they'd say, or "Okay, okay," which puzzled me. Were they asking me if I was okay? Telling me that they were okay? I just wasn't sure. But I did get the feeling that they had been trained from a very young age to be polite to tourists.

"Do you want to take my picture?" a little girl with at least a dozen red and blue and green plastic baubles in her hair asked me.

The laundromat had turned into a hair salon by the time I got back. The woman who owns the place had moved one of the plastic chairs from inside out onto the front porch. In it sat a young man, his hair brushed straight up in the air. She was applying some kind of goo to it and braiding it into tiny cornrows.

"Looking good!" I said as I passed.

"Look better soon." He grinned.

I moved our clothes from the washers to the dryers, inserted more quarters, then leaned against one of the dryers, looked out the window. There were steps carved out of the stone going down to the water, and a dock. We could have landed there and saved ourselves some hauling. There was a blue and white fishing boat at anchor just off the dock, bobbing gently in the waves. The water was so clear you could see the concrete block the boat was tied to, could see the shadow of the boat clearly on the sandy bottom. I was doing laundry in paradise.

I WAS SCARED of Mom's wringer washer—all of us kids were.

"Stay back," Mom would say as she fished the clothes out of the steaming water with a wooden spoon and fed them through the wringers. "If your arm gets caught in the wringers, your bones will be crushed."

This puzzled me — I'd seen the wringers pop apart when she tried to feed too many clothes through. Surely an arm, even a kid's arm, would trigger the safety release. But we stayed back.

Mom continued to use her wringer washer long after everyone else's mother had moved to an automatic.

"I don't trust them," she'd say. "And they use too much water."

Mom would start boiling water for the whites as soon as Dad left for work. She would actually boil enough water to fill the tub, add detergent and a cup of bleach, stir it with her wooden spoon. She wouldn't use the agitator, because without clothes in the tub, it splashed too much. She didn't want to risk getting bleach water on her apron or, worse, in her eyes, or ours.

"Stand back," she'd say, as she stirred cautiously.

Then she'd add the whites, poke them down, set the timer for ten minutes, let them agitate while she sipped her now-cold coffee, run them through the wringers when the timer went off. The rest of the clothes would follow, according to colour and level of grime. The tea towels and tablecloth came next, then the sheets, then the bath towels, then our underwear and shirts, then our muddy pants. Sometimes she'd wash our running shoes before she drained the machine and filled it again to repeat the whole process for the rinse.

It took her until midmorning to finish the washing. Then she'd haul everything out to the backyard, give each item a fierce shake and hang it on our flimsy inverted-umbrella clothesline. She would discreetly hang our underwear behind the towels and sheets, but I was mortified at having it out there at all. I didn't understand why we couldn't get a dryer like everyone else.

"Uses too much electricity," Mom would say.

When I left home, the first thing I bought myself was an apartment-sized washer and dryer, which I hauled from place to place. No way I was going to use a wringer washer, and there was something shameful, it seemed to me, about going to a laundromat. Too public. Too many bored people waiting for their clothes to dry, nothing better to do than watch you fold your not-quite-clean tea towels.

Now I seek them out—all that hot water, and dryers that leave the towels nice and fluffy. So much better than washing things in salt water in a pail, rinsing them in the smallest amount of fresh water possible, hanging them from the rigging to dry. On a good day, you don't have to retrieve your bedsheets from the water and start all over again.

I understand now, in a way I didn't then, that perhaps my mother wasn't just backwards. Maybe she took pleasure in doing laundry the way she'd always done it, the way her mother taught her. I remember watching her patiently fish our little socks out of the water and feed them through the wringers one by one. She would linger as she folded our corduroy pants and plaid shirts, shook the wrinkles out of our Sunday dresses, tied the ribbons at the back into pretty bows. She always smiled as she smoothed the baby's sleepers, folded the flannel blankets with bunnies on them. And there was no mistaking the satisfaction on her face as she carried the baskets of clean laundry into the house.

I have trouble reconciling this version of my mother, so content with her small life, so fearful of everything—with the woman who understood my decision to go sailing, who pushed me away, in fact. I had been dreading going to the home to tell her that I was thinking of going sailing with Chris. But she didn't hesitate for a minute. She put her good hand on my chest, pushed me, hard.

"Go!" she said. "Go."

WHEN THE LAUNDRY was dry, folded, and packed back into the plastic bags, I hauled it out onto the back porch, planning to sit on the stone steps and watch for Chris. Perhaps I could wave him in to the dinghy dock, save us lugging our laundry back through the town.

Outside the door, two women stood talking. Well, one was talking, the other was listening. The one doing the talking wore a brightly coloured dress, red and blue and orange, and was holding a bible in her hands. The other woman had a baby on her hip and was wearing a white blouse, a red skirt, and a wide-brimmed hat with elaborate trim. She looked like she had just come from church. They stopped talking, turned and looked at me. Uh-oh, I thought.

"Hello," I said.

"Okay? Okay?" the one with the bible sang out. She looked out over the harbour. "Where ya boat?"

"It's in Staniel," I explained. "I've just come here to do my wash."

"May I pray wit you?" she asked.

There was no getting around it. She tucked her bible under her arm, took both my hands. Both women closed their eyes. I stared at the baby. The baby stared at me.

"Lord, we t'ank you for dis woman, dis beautiful woman. We t'ank you for bringing her to our beautiful islands, the mos beautiful islands in the world."

"Amen," the other woman murmured.

"T'ank you for dis woman, and keep she safe on the water, keep she safe on she boat, keep all a ya on the boats safe, on ah own beautiful water."

"Hear her," the woman in the hat agreed.

The baby was still staring at me. I lowered my eyes.

"Lord, bless dis woman, dis beautiful woman, and keep she safe. Amen."

"Amen," murmured the other woman.

"Amen," I said.

They opened their eyes and smiled at me. The woman was still holding my hands.

"Thank you," I said, squeezing her hands and releasing them gently. "Thank you."

And I really meant it.

THE SECOND SQUALL has come and gone. I stand in the companionway where I'm safely (I hope) surrounded by wood. Chris studies the radar.

"There's good news and bad news. The good news is I can see the other side of the next squall and it looks like it's the last one. The bad news is it's four miles wide."

I brace myself for the worst. How can four miles of thunderstorms pass over us without at least one direct strike? Never get caught out on the water in a thunderstorm, I can hear my mother saying. You'll get hit for sure. Never stand under a tree. Or anywhere outside, for that matter. Lightning can travel through wet ground, strike you dead before you know it. Not that you're safe inside. Don't ever touch an aluminum window. Or stand near the stove. Or the sink. Or worse, between the two. If lightning hits the house, a fireball will come out of the stove and arc to the sink. Go to the basement. Stay there. It's the only safe place.

*You're just like your mother. Afraid of everything. Why don't you go down below, pull the covers up over your head?*

After the first half hour, I find myself releasing my death grip on the sides of the companionway and even watching the lightning rather than squeezing my eyes closed at every flash. The wind is fierce, the rain torrential, but they are nothing compared to the lightning. A deafening crash, then a jagged streak of light, how close now? I start to count, one thousand, two... I never get past two. The storm is right on us. Lightning strikes the water to the left of the boat, to the right, leaving us completely blinded between flashes. It's terrifying. But it's also really quite beautiful, in a holy-cow-I-wish-I-were-watching-this-on-TV kind of way.

Bless this woman, I keep repeating to myself. Bless this man. Keep them safe on the water, the beautiful water.

Something happens during that first storm at sea. I find myself surrendering—what else can I do? I feel very small out in the wide ocean, in the violent storm. But I feel something else, I feel free somehow. And it's a kind of release. There's nothing I can do.

## May 27

*Day 6*

The next day we're gliding over glassy seas. The storm has completely flattened out the waves—when you look over the side, you can see your reflection in the deep blue water. My hair is getting long and, for some reason, falls into curls at sea, long brown ringlets. Is that really me? That woman looks so happy.

The wind is so light that even with the spinnaker up, we're barely holding three knots. But every now and then a gentle gust pushes us up to four. It's enough.

We're both pretty tired. The storm last night completely messed up our watch schedule. It let up just after midnight, and Chris insisted on taking the first watch—he was still on full alert, I think. I slept fitfully for maybe an hour, then I made us a couple of mugs of milky tea and we sat together watching the clouds disappear in the distance, watching the stars slowly emerge. It was just getting light when Chris finally went down. He slept through breakfast, then I slept through lunch, and now it's late afternoon and neither of us is sleepy.

I've washed my hair in the rainwater that filled the bucket tied to the radar arch—this makes me very happy, for some reason—and I'm lounging against the sailbag on the foredeck, letting the wind dry my hair. I should get out of the sun, but not yet, not yet.

I close my eyes, listen to the murmur of the bow wave, the whisper of the spinnaker as it fills, then relaxes, fills, then relaxes. Dad would love this.

I DON'T THINK Dad was meant be a family man. The urge to run away was always strong in him. When he was a little boy, his family lived briefly in a rented house on Victoria Street in Kitchener. When he got tired of playing with an old railway spike in the dirt in the backyard, he would sit on the curb in front of the house and watch the streetcars crest the hill on Victoria, disappear from view, then reappear a few minutes later in the distance. If he had a nickel, I think he would have risked his mother's wrath and boarded one. But he grew up during the Depression, no one had any money, least of all his parents. His father was on relief, and struggled to feed his growing family and keep a roof over their heads. They moved from one place to another, sometimes in the middle of the night. Each was worse than the last.

One day Dad came out of school to find his father waiting outside the gate.

"Come on," he said, and took him to their newest place, an apartment in a tenement above a Greek restaurant and a fish market on King Street. The building was old, dark, and dingy, the once-varnished front stairs layered with dust and grime. At the top of the stairs was a windowless corridor, dirty grey walls just visible by the light of dim bulbs strung out along the high ceiling. The apartment itself was bright enough, though — long and narrow with windows overlooking the street. The Capitol Theatre was right next door, and at night, Dad would fall asleep in the bed he shared with one of his brothers, bathed in light, then plunged into darkness as the marquee flashed on and off.

But this was much better than their previous place, which had been completely overrun with cockroaches.

No wonder Dad dreamed of escaping. In high school, he figured out a way to get to the ocean, if he could just get his hands on a little boat. He had traced a line in his geography book from the Grand River in Kitchener to Lake Erie, across the lake and into the Erie Canal, then down the canal and out the Hudson River to the Atlantic. I'm not sure what he thought he'd do once he got there. But he never did.

When he finished high school, he took a job as a transmitter operator at the local radio station, then was offered a job as an engineer at a station in Niagara Falls. There he met Mom, and as soon as they were married, the babies started coming. That's all she had ever wanted in life—babies. They moved back to Kitchener and in with his parents, and that was the end of his dreams.

Dad joined the army in order to support his growing family, and Mom moved with his parents to a cottage in Wasaga Beach. Mom, a timid young bride, pregnant now with her second child—me—tried to stay out of Grandma's way.

"Yes, Mother," I can hear her saying. "Peggy—take off your shoes! I'll sweep that up, Mother."

I can picture Mom heaving herself to her feet, Grandma standing at the screen door, arms crossed, a frown on her face.

There is a picture of me sitting in a high chair outside the cottage, wearing only my diapers—and a big smile. My face and arms and stomach are smeared with cottage cheese, and there's some in my hair. I'll bet Mom got in trouble for that. A later picture shows Peggy and me sitting on the cement slab in front of the cottage, wearing matching dresses Grandma made for us out of some leftover curtain material, hard black shoes, white ankle socks. Our hair is tightly braided. There. That's more like it.

Not that Grandma was always old and sour. She was born on a farm in Minnesota in 1892, one of sixteen children. Like many Swedish immigrants, her parents decided to move to California, where the weather was better and farming much easier. When she was old enough, she was sent to work for a respectable Swedish family, but she ran off to San Francisco. She was working as a telephone operator at a hotel when she met my grandpa and they were married shortly after.

I have a picture of the two of them taken around that time. They're sitting together on the running board of a Model A Ford with "MADRONE RODEO July 4-5-6" painted on the side of it. Grandma's hands are folded demurely on her lap, but shockingly, she's wearing loose bloomers tucked into stockings that come up to her knees.

She's a stout woman, with legs like a pool table's. Her tiny feet are squeezed into a pair of dusty boots. She has a loose bandana around her neck, tied at the back, red, I think, though the photograph is black and white. I think she's dressed as a cowgirl. All that's missing is the hat.

Her hair is cropped short—in itself scandalous, I'm sure. Tight finger curls frame her broad face She's looking at something off to the side, smiling broadly. Grandpa sits beside her, looking almost clownish in a suit that's way too big for him. You can see a big hole in the bottom of one of his boots. He's holding a top hat in one hand, a fat cigar in the other. He too is smiling. They both look so happy. I wonder what happened.

I know some of the story—Grandpa goes to the school in the middle of the day and collects the children, takes them home. For some reason, Grandma is sitting on a chair in the dining room with her back to the wall. Grandpa walks into the bedroom and comes out with a shotgun, puts the gun to her chest, tells her calmly that he's going to shoot her first, then the children, then himself, unless she agrees to move to Canada. Which she does.

After that, according to my dad, their relationship was more of an armed truce than a marriage.

It was a happy day for my parents when Dad was discharged from the army, now trained as an x-ray technician, and the two of them could set up housekeeping together. Far away from his parents.

But he went back to visit from time to time, like a dutiful son. He tells the story of watching them play Scrabble after dinner one night, sitting at the scrubbed wooden table, an ashtray between them, Grandpa with a glass of whisky in front of him. Grandma put down a word.

"What the hell is that?"

Grandma looked at him coolly.

"It's another word for a prisoner, Louis."

Grandpa studied the board, finally put all his letters down.

"What is that supposed to be?"

"A pimple on a goose's ass," he said, getting up from the table.

Another night Dad arrived to find his father drinking pretty hard. Grandma had already gone to bed, and Grandpa decided that he wanted something to eat. A friend of his owned a restaurant in town, and even though it was late and the restaurant would be closed, Grandpa knew his friend would open up for him.

Grandpa opened the bedroom door. "I'm going to get a hamburger," he said. "I'll bring one back for you."

"I don't want a damned hamburger," Grandma replied. "What time is it?"

"I'm bringing you a hamburger."

"Well, I don't want one."

Dad went with Grandpa, who was too drunk to be out on his own. And sure enough, Grandpa brought a hamburger back for Grandma.

"Here's your hamburger," he said to the darkened room.

"I don't want the damned thing," she said.

"Well, I'll put it here on the dresser."

"It can stay there till hell freezes over," she said.

And it did. The next time Dad visited, it was still there. Neither of them would throw it out.

I WATCH A pair of tropicbirds drift lazily towards us, long white tailfeathers trailing behind, funny little legs and feet tucked in tight. I can clearly see the black masks and bright orange bills as they scan the water for fish. One of them spreads its wings wide, hovers for a minute—has he seen something?—then lands gently on the water beside the boat, rises and falls with the swell. His mate lands beside him.

I rouse myself from the sail bag, look back at Chris, sprawled in the cockpit, reading his book. He looks up, smiles.

"Time for dinner?" he says hopefully.

As I walk back towards the cockpit, something catches my eye in the distance. A dolphin arcing out of the water, bounding towards us. There is another one not far behind, and another, and another.

"Look, Chris!"

He joins me at the bow. There must be thirty of them in all, racing to see who will get to us first. Next thing we know the water around the boat is churning with dolphins, playing in the bow wave, swimming along beside us. These aren't the bottlenose dolphins we usually see. They're much larger, and these dolphins have dark backs, almost black, and white sides, which we can see clearly as they leap out of the water for the sheer joy of it. They tilt their heads slightly as they swim by, fix a dark, shining eye on us. Watch this! Watch what I can do! Or maybe, come on in!

Then, as if on command, they suddenly swim off. We watch them disappear in the distance.

"Dolpin TV," says Chris, with a smile.

AT DUSK, THE wind dies altogether. We have no choice but to motor. We leave the main up to catch the occasional slight breeze, but most of the time the sail just flutters uselessly.

So far we've been sailing north in order to take advantage of ocean currents and the prevailing winds from the west. Having the wind on the beam — as opposed to beating into it or sailing downwind — is our most comfortable point of sail. We're also trying to avoid the big calm section in the middle of the North Atlantic, but now I'm wondering if we've strayed a little too far east.

Chris reassures me that we're fine, right on course. I look at the chart plotter, which is still just a blank screen with the words *Atlantic Ocean* written across it, and I raise an eyebrow. He goes below, comes back up with our pilot chart of the North Atlantic, checks our latitude and longitude, then makes a little "x" on the chart.

"We're right here," he says. "Now you go and sleep — it's my watch."

JUST BEFORE MIDNIGHT, I am jolted awake by a screaming sound coming from the engine room. I leap out of bed and fling the engine room door open, looking for flames or maybe water rushing in — it sounds that catastrophic. The screaming stops when Chris shuts the engine off. He grabs a flashlight, pushes past me, dives into the inner workings of the engine.

"I think it's the thrust bearing," he says as he strips off his T-shirt. "Hand me that trouble light. And please go and try to keep the boat steady."

This is easier said than done. We are dead in the water. Fortunately, the seas are almost flat so we just bob gently. I make tiny corrections, trying to keep the boat from wallowing around. The last thing we need right now is for Chris to get seasick.

He's down there for a long time. I have to resist the urge to go down and ask how he's doing. But I can hear him banging away at something, so I know he's okay. I look up at the fluttering sail, wonder if dropping it would make things better or worse.

Finally the engine room door opens and Chris emerges. The thrust bearing has been a problem right from the start of this journey, but it's not the thrust bearing this time. The propeller shaft won't budge. Clearly something is wrapped around the prop.

"I'll have to dive on it in the morning," he says, wiping the grease from his hands on a paper towel. He can see the horror on my face. "Don't worry, there won't be any sharks this far out," he adds, not very convincingly.

Chris goes down to sleep and I start my watch. There isn't much to do — no sails to tend, no gauges to keep an eye on. No sense plotting our position, even — if we're wandering off course, there's nothing I can do about it. At one point, I see a light off our stern — a fishing boat, I'm sure of it. Maybe they do long-line fishing out here, maybe we've snagged one of their lines and we're trailing chunks of bait behind us. The sea will be swimming with sharks.

I look through the binoculars. It's just a sailboat heading for Bermuda.

It's going to be a long night.

We've seen sharks, of course. We saw several in the clear, shallow waters of the Bahamas, but we've never had a close encounter with one — unless you count the shark that took our fish as we sailed out of the cut in Antigua. The fiercest creature we've had first-hand experience with is a barracuda. We were snorkelling happily around a coral head in Staniel Cay, admiring all the pretty fish, when suddenly they scattered. A large, snake-like fish had come from behind the coral head and positioned itself between us and the nervous little fish, who were now hiding in crevices in the coral. It was a handsome creature, dark blue on top, silver on the bottom, with silver and black spots along its sides.

But I wasn't paying much attention to its colouring—I was looking at its teeth, sharp fangs in a jaw that seemed to go on forever. Chris swam in for a closer look. The fish lunged towards him. They were fang to mask.

I'm not sure how I got there, exactly, but next thing I knew I was in the dinghy. I must have catapulted myself out of the water. Chris wasn't far behind.

"What was that?"

Our first barracuda, we discovered when we looked it up in our guide. Ferocious predators who don't like people messing with their food supply. Chris was lucky to get away with all his fingers.

IN THE MORNING, once the sun is well overhead, Chris puts on his mask and flippers and lowers himself carefully into the water, not wanting to attract any more attention than necessary. I lean anxiously over the rail, watch his descent. I'm amazed at how clear the dark blue water is. Shafts of sunlight disappear into the depths, lighting the water around him. I can see him sharply even when he's six feet under. He keeps turning his head, scanning for sharks as he inspects the prop. He returns to the surface almost immediately.

"There are three little fish under the boat," he says. "Blue and green, very pretty."

Then we both realize what this means. Dead in the water just a few hours and already we're becoming a floating ecosystem. Little fish come, then big fish, then bigger fish. He dives again, is down longer than I think possible. He's under the boat now and I can't see him.

What if he doesn't come up? What if he's knocked his head on the hull or passed out from holding his breath for too long? What do I do? I look at the Lifesling tied to the radar arch. I haven't studied the instructions on the bag closely, but I know that the thing to do is get the Lifesling around him somehow and winch him aboard.

Then what? What if he's hurt? Or worse? We have antibiotics and antibiotic cream on board, a skin stapler (and a staple remover), and lots of bandages. Lots. I took a first aid course for offshore sailors before we left, practiced stapling an orange (very like human skin… except, obviously, for the colour). I learned how to deal with some of the more common injuries at sea—a screwdriver in the lung, for example (never stand at the foot of the mast when someone is working overhead). Don't try to remove the screwdriver—just cover it with sterile bandages and call for medical evacuation.

The course almost scared me off sailing altogether. If someone dies at sea, we were told, put them in the dinghy and cover them with coffee grounds to hide the smell. I think we have enough coffee on board to do that. They didn't say whether you should use fresh or used coffee grounds. Fresh, I hope. By the time I drank enough coffee to cover Chris with wet grounds, a dead body would be the least of my problems.

Suddenly he surfaces.

"Bolt cutters," he says grimly.

It takes him a long time. He dives, then surfaces again, clings to the swim ladder for a minute while he catches his breath, dives again. Fifteen minutes and many dives later, he comes up and hands me the bolt cutters, then dives again and surfaces with a huge ball of nylon rope and some shredded fishing net. It's at least two feet in diameter. So there are fishermen out here. And sharks, I presume.

I'm glad when he's safely back on board. And so is he.

He's exhausted and smudged with bottom paint, which is full of toxic chemicals that discourage things from growing on the under-side of the boat. I help him wash it off, scrubbing him down with dish soap and rinsing him with pails of seawater. Then I send him down for a nap.

He's asleep in no time, apparently none the worse for his misadventure. In fact, he's smiling slightly. He's clean now, from his swim, but he hasn't shaved since we left Antigua, his chin is covered with dark stubble. His hair has more grey in it than when I met him and curls a little at the nape of his neck. He needs a haircut, I suppose, but I like his hair a little longer. It makes him look like the bad boy he must have been when he was younger.

He's told me stories of hot-wiring his father's car and taking it for a joyride in the middle of the night when he was just fourteen. Then he got his own car, which he tinkered with until it would run, borrowing parts from his father's car as necessary, sometimes remembering to put them back. Then he got a motorcycle, which wasn't licensed (neither was he), but that didn't stop him from tearing up the highway on it. In time he got an MG. Then a sailboat. Then he discovered airplanes.

He's a man who has to move. No wonder he's so happy sailing across an ocean. He looks ten years younger when we're at sea.

At the moment, I probably look ten years older. What if I had seen a shark? Yelling wouldn't have done any good. I guess I could have banged on the hull, or thrown something overboard to get Chris's attention, but that would have brought the shark over to investigate. No, I would have been helpless. And utterly alone in the middle of the ocean.

*Well, what did you think was going to happen?*

*May 28*

~~~~~~~

*Day 7*

We're 300 miles southeast of Bermuda, too far east to sail there comfortably. The wind is coming from the northwest and we'd have to beat right into it to make landfall there. We've decided it's just not worth it for a couple of full nights' sleep and an armload of fresh produce. We've got lots of provisions on board, and water and fuel. If we hold this course, in another two or three days we'll be far enough north to make the turn towards the Azores.

But I'm in no hurry to head out into the middle of the North Atlantic. The sailing is so easy, our days so pleasant. It gets a little cool at night now, but by the time the sun comes up, it's warm enough for me to shed my fleece hoodie.

Quietly, so as not to wake Chris, I make coffee, taking the beans above deck to grind them. The smell of coffee usually wakes him, but if not, I get him up in time to check in with Chris Parker at 6:30. We set the sails for the morning — we always reduce sail at night — then have breakfast in the cockpit, reviewing the day's forecast, making our plans for the day.

Today I'm going to hang the bedding out to air, do a couple of Portuguese lessons, spray WD-40 on the porthole latches so I can close them quickly if I need to, and make some bread.

But the day has other plans for us.

My bread is in the oven, I've hung the sheets from the handrails on the ceiling in the salon where they'll catch the breeze that comes in through the portholes, and I'm just finishing my

Portuguese lessons when Chris calls from the foredeck where he's working.

"Better close up down there."

I close and latch the hatches and portholes, and by the time I come up on deck, there's a bank of rainclouds heading towards us. We can see sheets of rain slicing down. I get ready to release the main halyard so we can drop the sail.

"Wait," Chris says. "Let's try to sail around it."

We're getting pretty good at this. First we reduce sail in case we aren't successful. We reef the main as far as it will go, leaving just a small triangle of sail up, and reduce the genoa to just a slip. Then we tack out of the path of the squall. The wind is rising, so even though we have hardly any sail up, we move smartly along. Five knots. Six.

We almost make it—but we're caught by the trailing edge of the squall. The wind suddenly rises to thirty knots and we heel over sharply, then we're pelted with rain. But it's over quickly, and in no time, we have the sails re-set and we're back on course and feeling pretty smug.

"More coffee?" I ask.

"Sure."

The porthole latches can wait till tomorrow.

"So how are the Portuguese lessons going?" Chris asks, as we settle in with a fresh pot.

"I can now say 'The car is white' and 'A man is running.' That should come in handy, don't you think?"

"Maybe."

CHRIS HAS GONE down for a nap and I pour myself another cup of coffee and open my computer to write to Brenda. First I take a look around. Nothing on the horizon as far as the eye can see.

Well, Beek, it's another beautiful day at sea and we've just made the decision not to stop at Bermuda after all—we're heading straight for the Azores! Of course as soon as we decided this a squall appeared on the horizon, but we managed to sail around it. Aren't we clever??

You will be at a resort right now, stretched out on a lounge chair, I hope, with a good book and maybe a nice cold glass of wine. I can see the condensation running down the side of the glass from here... We never drink when we're on passage — not, of course, that I mind, or even think about it, no, not me. Chablis. I'd make mine a nice cold glass of Chablis.

Anna, you know, will be absolutely fine. She and Peggy will be strolling to the playground, Anna chatting away, Peggy listening patiently. Then a quiet supper together and bath and stories and Peggy will put a line through one more day on the calendar while Anna watches and they will count the days that are left and then Anna will drift happily off to sleep.

Speaking of stroking off the days...seven days at sea now, and all is well. That doesn't mean I don't still have my doubts about this enterprise. Shall I tell you about a dream I had the other night?? Ha ha ha! You don't have any choice.

You and I were standing on a hill, looking down at *MonArk* at anchor in a sandy cove below us. Chris was busy on deck, running flat lines of nylon webbing from bow to stern on either side of the deck.

"What's he doing?" you asked.

"Rigging the jack lines. It's the last thing we have to do before we set out in the ocean."

"What are they for?"

"They're something to clip our safety harnesses onto if we have to go forward at night or in big seas. I'm not so worried about getting swept overboard myself — Chris could turn the boat around and come back for me. I think. But if he goes over, I'm in trouble. And so is he."

I don't know what happened next, but suddenly the boat was sinking, Chris was nowhere to be seen, he was gone. As the boat settled, I could see in through the companionway, the new leather settee darkening as sea water poured in, the brass lantern on its side, a pool of oil spreading over the water that rose steadily. Water reached the portholes, the top of the companionway, and things began to float out: a blue jay feather, my well-worn biography of Vanessa Bell, my journal, open to where I left it on the table, pages fluttering in the wind. The photograph of Emily I keep tucked inside the front cover was carried away, up, up into the sky then gone.

As the boat went down, our things spread out over the water for all to see. A couple of dinner plates, a stained tea towel, our olivewood-handled corkscrew, a frying pan, the sleeping bag we use as a duvet on our bed, one pillow, then the other. Chris's fishing rod floated slowly away, spoon boy glinting in the sun. Soon, only the mast was visible. Then it too was gone. And Chris was gone, his red Antigua race week cap spinning in a slow circle where the boat had been.

A crowd had gathered on the beach below us. You took me firmly by the elbow, turned me away.

"Come," you said. "It's all gone."

What would I do, Beek? We've only been together for a short time, but already I can't imagine a life without Chris. May I never have to.

Time to take the bread out of the oven—yes, I'm making bread in the middle of the ocean. I started it first thing this morning, set the bowl of dough out on deck in the sun to rise while the oven heated up—it takes about an hour to get up to temperature. Once I put the bread in the oven, I had to keep a close eye on it. The oven has no temperature control, so I have to keep fiddling with it to keep it more or less in the 350 degree range. But it smells like it's done now. Fresh bread for lunch!

It's sunny again, Beek, and as warm as it's going to get today. I could oil the porthole latches, but I think I'll read the afternoon away, rest up for this evening's round of the Great Trans-Atlantic Backgammon Tournament. I am lagging sorely behind.

Love you.
Linda

AS I'M CLIMBING down the companionway ladder, I spot something huge and white looming behind us. It's a massive freighter just off our stern! How did it get there? I leap into the cockpit and punch it in on the radar, which is how we usually track the paths of ships. Then I realize that this guy is close enough for me to watch through my binoculars. When I'm satisfied he's going to pass safely behind us, I breathe a sigh of relief. How have I missed him in my admittedly haphazard scans of the horizon? I resolve to do better. I set my watch to beep every fifteen minutes to remind myself to look around.

As the ship disappears in the distance, I sit with the binoculars in my lap, scan the horizon dutifully every time my watch beeps — and holy cow, there's another big boat, coming from the other direction. It's a huge oil tanker, called *No Smoking*, as so many of them are. He's close enough for me to make out the lettering on his deckhouse.

As I watch the approaching tanker, I begin to understand why I've been caught off-guard — twice now. These ships really move when they're out in the ocean. In no time he's crossed our stern and is steaming over the horizon in the direction the first ship came from. Clearly we are crossing — or in — one of the major shipping lanes between Europe and North America.

The lazy first leg of our journey is over. We're going to have to keep a much sharper lookout now — which is actually quite pleasant. I've been missing a lot, spending my days with my nose buried in a book.

Four greater shearwaters land in our wake. Perhaps we bring fish to the surface? But I don't see them feeding at all. They just settle in, bob along behind us. Maybe they like our company? I try to think of four names that start with *Sh* — Shirley, Shelly, Sherman… Can't think of a fourth one. "Sorry, buddy," I murmur. Wait — Sheldon.

They are watching something in the sky above the boat. I look — a beautiful white-tailed tropicbird floats above us. The same one we saw before? Maybe it's following us, still looking for that squid?

*Beep.* I scan the horizon. Nothing.

Then it's my turn to nap. It's hot below deck, so I climb into the V-berth, open the hatch wide, and stretch out on my back beneath it, using the spinnaker we store below deck when it's not in use for a pillow. Above me the sails breathe in and out, in and out. The sun plays across my face as we rock gently along. I close my eyes. But I'm too happy to sleep.

Happy. Not something I expected to feel again.

THE FIRST FEW months in my condo were pretty grim. I didn't go out much, except to go to work. One morning, my car wouldn't start. A sharp wind drove fine pellets of ice against my face as I stood helplessly looking under the hood. I don't know what I was looking for.

"What's up?" Chris had come out to his car. "Geez, it's cold."

"My car won't start."

"Here, I'll give you a boost." He pulled a pair of jumper cables out of his trunk. It took a few tries, but finally my car started.

"Thanks, Chris. Now I can drive it to the dealer."

"Why? You just need a new battery." He put away the jumper cables, walked around to the passenger side of my car. "Come on, we'll go to Canadian Tire."

I was dumbstruck. He was going to help me?

*You're pathetic. Deal with this yourself.*

Half an hour later I was standing in the parking lot of Canadian Tire, hands burrowed in my pockets, watching as Chris hooked up my new battery.

"Stand beside me," he said, "You'll be out of the wind."

EASTER WEEKEND I ventured to the woods for the first time. I'd never gone alone without Chester, my husband's big bull mastiff. I kept looking around, half expecting him to come crashing through the underbrush, ears flapping, a big string of drool hanging from his chin. I had hung a picture of Chester on the wall above Emily's bowl, at eye level for her. She misses him, I'd tell people.

Emily looked very small as she trundled along the path ahead of me. She kept stopping and looking back at me. Are you sure this is a good idea?

The woods were perfectly silent, not a bird to be heard. I checked the pond — no ducks. Then I spotted a wood duck in a tree on the far side, it must be nesting close by. Yes, there was a cavity in the trunk, just below where the bird was perched. It was too early in the year for the fledglings to be leaving the nest, but I watched for a while, just in case. When they're just a day old, they climb up the inside of the nest and fling themselves over the side, landing in the water, if they're lucky — on hard ground, if they're not.

As spring turned to summer, instead of eating bagged salad every night, I began walking to the restaurant up the street and getting takeout salad — spinach, pear, and gorgonzola was my favourite. I'd arrange it on one of my good plates, and instead of eating in front of the TV, watching reruns of *Friends*, I'd pour myself a glass of wine and eat at the table, watching the sun set. It would wash the room in gold light, picking out certain objects — the glass vase full of purple hyacinths, a bird's nest, my new two-volume biography of Colette in its beautiful pale yellow binding.

Driving home from work one Friday in June, I found myself thinking, I can do whatever I want this weekend, go wherever I want — no one knows where I am, no one cares. A couple of months ago, this thought would have reduced me to tears. Now it felt kind of good.

I went to a movie alone for the first time in my life, watched a film about a housewife who ran away to Venice, where she found work in a flower shop and started playing the accordion again, and dancing, things she'd given up when she married a man who sold plumbing fixtures.

Later that night, I was awakened by a cat in the garden below my bedroom window. She would cry out loudly, just long enough to make her need known, then give a couple of polite, quiet, almost apologetic meows. Traffic passed by in the background, either oblivious or indifferent to her cries. But I was listening.

SUMMER CAME AND my condo started to feel a little small. I would throw all the windows open, let the sun and fresh air in. On the

July long weekend, I had the old school to myself—everyone else had left town—so I poured myself a glass of wine and went and sat on the back step. A bank of thunderclouds was rolling in, but I was sheltered in the big brick arch over the door. Emily sat beside me, ears up, keeping an eye on the sky. She would look at my face from time to time. You can feel the rain coming, right? I stroked her ears reassuringly as I sipped my wine, watched the sky darken. This is enough, I thought. This is enough.

But it wasn't enough for long.

Emily and I started going for long rambles in the country. I'd get up early, put on my hiking boots, make myself a thermos of coffee and a peanut butter sandwich, grab a couple of oranges and my binoculars. Our first stop was the river just outside Cambridge. We'd park at the rowing club and walk along the trail to the top of the cliffs, keeping an eye out for osprey. After that we'd drive to the woods behind Langdon Hall, hop the fence and wander along the deer trails. Once we startled a young deer coming the other way. Neither of us knew what to do, exactly. I stepped off the trail into the thick underbrush and let it pass.

When the sun was directly overhead, I'd eat my lunch sitting on a boulder overlooking the meadows, stretch out in the long grass for a nap, while Emily kept watch. Then I'd drive to the conservation area, follow the trail through the pine trees, around the shallow lakes, up the hill into the maple forest, back around the lakes. I'd watch the swallows skimming the water, catching bugs.

I used to like to watch the barn swallows at the farm trying to coax their fledglings into flight. The young birds would teeter on the clothesline outside my kitchen window, flap their wings as their parents swooped overhead, feed me, feed me. No, come fly with me, it's easy, you can catch your own bugs.

Our last stop of the day would be Indian Lookout, where I'd sit on the damp ground, feet dangling over the edge of the bluff, eating my last orange as I watched the light in the river valley begin to fade. Once a bald eagle flew by, just below me, then circled back so close I didn't need my binoculars. Enough, I said to myself. Surely this is enough.

Some nights when I got home, I'd find a message from Brenda on my answering machine.

"Where have you been? I've been calling you all weekend."

I didn't tell her I'd been out trespassing and sleeping in meadows.

"HAVEN'T SEEN MUCH of you this summer," I said.

Chris and I were sitting on the back steps, Emily asleep in the sun at our feet. The weather was still warm, but the leaves had started to turn. The roses and peonies had given way to purple coneflowers and black-eyed susans.

"I've been up at the boat."

"All summer?"

"Yep."

"I don't get this boat thing. Tell me about it."

"Better. I'll show you some pictures." He went upstairs and returned minutes later with a photo album.

"My first boat was a Hughes 25."

He showed me a picture of a trim little sailboat, gazed at it longingly.

"But I had to sell it when the kids started coming." He furrowed his brow. "I'm not sure why. The MG had to go too."

After his divorce he bought a Grampion 30, which seemed huge to him.

"I was getting ready to sail to the Caribbean in it, had installed a staysail rig and running backstays, but then I saw this—"

He showed me a picture of a much bigger boat. He had been sailing in Lake Erie, heading for Port Stanley, when he was passed by a big steel sailboat with beautiful lines. He'd always wanted a steel boat.

"Fibreglass is great for sailing around in the Great Lakes, but in uncharted waters, a steel boat provides greater security. It's also a lot more stable."

To his surprise, when he arrived in Port Stanley, it was docked at the marina there. Everyone knew the boat. It was built there by a guy named Marv, who had just come back from the Caribbean and was looking to sell it.

"When Marv took me below and I saw the amazing job he had done on the woodwork, it was a done deal."

The name on the hull was *Thursday's Child*, but in later pictures, it was *MonArk*.

"You changed the name?" I said. "*MonArk*? First person singular? The animals go two by two, you know."

"I know that," he said sadly.

I WAS DREADING my first Christmas alone, fretting about whether or not to decorate my condo. I couldn't bear the thought of a tree. Maybe a big poinsettia?

Then there was Chris at the door, with a beautiful poinsettia. His daughter's swim team had been selling them to raise money and he'd bought half a dozen.

"Here," he said, handing it to me without ceremony.

I put it on my dining room table. It was just right.

Christmas Day dawned sunny and cold. I had it all planned, had even laid out my clothes the night before. As soon as I opened my eyes, I jumped out of bed, pulled my fleecies over my pyjamas, put on my warmest outdoor clothes, including the mad bomber hat my husband hated so much, and pulled on my big clumsy boots with the thick felt liners. I extracted a reluctant Emily from the burrow of blankets at the foot of the bed, packed her in the car, and headed off to the conservation area at the edge of town.

We made our way across the meadow, Emily pushing through new-fallen snow up to her chest, looking back at me from time to time. Was this a good idea? I thought we would be the only ones out walking on Christmas morning, but a single set of bootprints told me that some solitary walker had been there before us. When we reached the creek, I was surprised to see that it hadn't frozen over yet. I stood on the little wooden bridge, watched the cold, black water rushing by below me.

I plucked some dried leaves off a beech tree beside the creek and dropped them into the water one by one, watching them until they either sank or disappeared around the bend. I thought about the first Christmas on the farm, unwrapping a pair of leather work boots with a bottle of Chanel tucked into them, remembered giving the sheep an extra armful of hay so we wouldn't have to go out and do chores after Christmas dinner. I watched the last leaf float out of sight and felt sad, but a little lighter somehow.

I spent the evening listening to Bach's cello suites and rearranging the shelves in the living room. I put my collection of Edward Gorey books within easy reach of my armchair, arranged all my bird nests on one shelf, along with my collection of feathers and a couple of almost-perfect robins' eggs. I put all the biographies of women I admire on another shelf, along with the books they had written, left the ones I didn't particularly admire where they were. I dug some pictures out of a box in my closet — my mother, a baby sleeping in the curve of a violin, Virginia Woolf in her mother's wedding dress — and stood them together on a shelf, placing a gold raku pear in front of them. I put a bowl of wild rosehips above the fireplace, scattered a handful of walnuts I had gathered in the woods around it, and sat back and admired my handiwork.

Then I poured myself a glass of wine, settled into my armchair with the paper, turned to the horoscope page and found mine.

*The biggest human temptation is to settle for too little. Don't.*


THE NEXT TIME I saw Chris he was loading boxes into his car. A lot of them.

"What's up?"

"I'm moving out."

Oh no, I thought.

He didn't look like he wanted to talk. I just waited, something I'd learned from him. He put down the box he was trying to jam into his already-full trunk.

"Cindy doesn't have time for a boyfriend," he said, leaning against the car. "I knew that when I met her."

"Where will you go?"

"I'm not sure. I'll find some place to stay for the winter, then in the spring I'll move onto the boat."

He looked up at the sky, not a cloud in sight, the kind of cold, clear day you get in January.

"Wind from the north," he said.

"How do you know?"

"The flag on that building —" he pointed. "You should come sailing with me sometime."

"I'd like that."

I HAD NEVER been on a sailboat before, was baffled by all the ropes, as I called them, not knowing a sheet from a halyard. Chris had me take the wheel as we motored out of the harbour and went forward to remove the sail cover. I watched him working on the foredeck. He'd stop from time to time, check our heading — "a little more to the right" — look around for other boats.

"Ready to raise sail?" he asked.

"What do I do?"

"Just keep the boat pointing into the wind."

I could do that. In no time, he had the mainsail up. It fluttered weakly in the gentle breeze. So this is sailing? He came back and took the helm, and as we rounded the lighthouse and left the shelter of the harbour, the sail suddenly filled with wind and we picked up speed. He handed me a rope — "Make sure that feeds out and doesn't get caught on anything, especially your foot" — and reached over and unfurled what I now know is the genoa, sheeting it in with one hand as he steered.

Then he switched the engine off and the only sound you could hear was water rushing along the hull and the occasional cry of a gull. We were galloping through the sparkling blue water, wind in our hair. Free, I thought. I'm free.

"You like it?" he said.

"I love it."

Chris was watching the sails, adjusting the heading a little to the left, a little to the right, making the most of the gentle wind. We were just two big kids, playing outside.

"WHAT DOES A guy have to do to get some dinner around here?"

"Okay, Captain Bligh."

We're still just two big kids, I think, as I climb out of the V-berth. I rummage in the fridge, decide to heat up some leftover boat gorp.

"This is my favourite," Chris says, licking his fork clean. "Except, of course, for canned stew."

"Why do I bother?" I say, throwing my hands up in the air. "Canned stew it is, from here to the Azores. God knows we have enough."

We get the boat ready for the night then Chris goes down for his pre-watch nap. The sky is absolutely clear, not a cloud in sight. I watch the sun inch towards the sharp blue horizon, then suddenly plunge out of sight. Why does it do that? I scan the horizon — nothing as far as the eye can see.

*"And you couldn't see a city on that marbled bowling ball,"* I sing softly to myself. *"Or a highway or a forest or me here, least of all."*

I am very small out here, but it feels good. For the first time in my life, I feel like there's enough room for me.

# THE CROSSING

On the first of June, we make the turn towards the Azores and the weather immediately gets colder, the sailing much rougher. The wind has suddenly gone east and is on the nose now. Instead of taking the seas on the quarter, we're pounding into them. And there is only a sliver of a moon left to light our way at night.

M is for Maude, who was swept out to sea, I think as I fret about the approaching dark. I check and double check the flashlight batteries, make sure we have everything we need in the cockpit—flashlight, binoculars, iPod, warm blanket, thermos of coffee, snacks, flashlight, where is the flashlight.

As Chris naps, I watch the light slowly fade, then open my computer to read Brenda's response to my last email, which I downloaded earlier in the day. One last look around, then I start reading.

Dear Linda,

Wow, that was quite a dream. And of course you have doubts—I would worry about you if you didn't.

Remember my trip to Sweden, my first big trip anywhere? I went—fled?—at a time when my marriage was a mess and I was struggling with so much confusion and pain. I just wanted to see my dear friend from school who had moved back home.

The anxiety started before I got to the airport. I felt sick about leaving the apartment (what if the plants died?), about checking in (what if my luggage got lost?), and about everything (what if I fall asleep during the stopover and miss my connecting flight?). By the time I arrived I was miserable.

Sweden is beautiful but I saw none of it, really, because I was so worried about something going disastrously wrong.

On the afternoon of the third day we were sitting on a dock in Stockholm. I was swinging my feet over the edge, looking at the skyline but really just feeling anxious and miserable (what a dreadful guest I must have been). As I looked down at the deep water I was struck with the horrifying thought that one of my new sandals could have slipped off into the water! What was I thinking? The misery that had become so familiar surged until I had a different thought.

So what? I would lose a sandal. Big deal.

The thought was so radical that it made me giddy. So I went for broke: I thought, I could drop my sandals in the ocean and it wouldn't matter. Heck, I could lose my purse and it wouldn't matter. I could throw my passport off the train, throw everything I own in the ocean, and it wouldn't matter. I would still be here. I might cause a little inconvenience at the embassy. I might need to borrow some sandals. But I would still be me, here. Everything in the world could be lost to me, and I would still be me.

I realized I was having a terrible time because I had packed everything for the trip, except myself. I had forgotten to bring my self, the one thing that I know and love and cannot be lost. In a split second, every scrap of worry and misery disappeared and the rest of the two weeks was fantastic.

So even if the boat went down and Chris were lost at sea, you would still be you. That's all any of us really has. Relationships, material things — they come and go. And we carry on.

But enough of that. You have a sturdy boat and Chris knows what he's doing. Remember that. And know that you don't have to be out in the middle of the ocean to get into trouble...

Anna had a big adventure at riding this week. She was riding unassisted, got distracted by the older girls, and let her pony noodle about. Well, apparently her pony thought that he was in his own custody (I am sure he cannot feel Anna on his back, when Anna is not providing any control) so he decided to rid himself of the pesky saddle by lying down and rolling! Anna waited as the pony made his leisurely way to the sawdust floor of the arena, then as soon as he was down on the ground and just getting ready to roll, she leaped from his back, timing it perfectly—like stepping off an escalator, or like Stephen Maturin waiting for the roll of the ship to climb up the side.

Needless to say there was much yelling and running about, but I remained pretty calm. I could see she had done right and as long as I did not let my imagination get away with me, it was done and fine. Anna was very cool and calm about it, shrugging off the attention of the instructor and the older girls. I was quite proud of her. Must admit that I replayed it a couple of times in the night, but otherwise it was fine. She now believes she is a real rider, since we always say you're not a rider until you fall off!

So you're on your way to the Azores. How exciting! How long till you make landfall? I'm glad the sailing has been easy—may it be so the whole way across.

Must go. I need to take Anna to pick up her new glasses, then dinner and bath and stories, then I have a graduate class to prepare for…tomorrow. No sense doing things too far in advance, I say.

Love you.
Beek

BRENDA'S LETTER HAS done nothing to make me feel any better. I close the computer, put my earbuds in. Listlessly, I scan the water around us in the failing light. What's that? There's something bobbing in the water just ahead of us, a triangle on a post about three feet high. It almost scrapes the side of the boat, we pass so close to it, but it's too dark to make out what it says. What's a sign doing out here in the middle of the ocean? Where did it come from? I fret about it until Chris comes up for his watch. Probably just a net marker come loose, he says. But I'm still uneasy.

Maybe the sign was a warning of some kind. Prepare to yield. Or perhaps it just marks the halfway point in our journey. We are now as far from Antigua as we are from the Azores. In other words, in the middle of nowhere. We can no longer raise Chris Parker on the SSB, though Chris tries each day, morning and night. We're on our own out here.

As I settle into the still-warm berth, I try not to think about the fact that bad things usually happen at night. The worst sailing we've had so far was the night we rounded Cape Fear. The Graveyard of the Atlantic, the waters off North Carolina are called, where the cold Labrador current and the warm Gulf Stream meet. It's an area of shifting sandbars, colliding waves, and unpredictable currents. And one of the highest densities of shipwrecks anywhere in the world.

THE WIND WAS from the southwest—we knew it would be, right on the nose, but it was supposed to clock around to the north, so we put out just a slip of genoa, reefed the main, and settled in for a lively sail. It was rough, but we soon got used to the pounding. You can handle almost anything on a nice sunny day.

But as the day wore on, the wind showed no sign of clocking and the seas continued to build. There was no way we could hold our course. By nightfall, we were sixty miles off shore, well off Cape Fear, but farther off shore than we'd ever been. And the wind was picking up.

We had crackers and cheese for supper—neither of us wanted to spend much time below deck, and in truth, we were both feeling a little queasy. Then I went down to try to sleep while Chris took the first watch. I lay there in the dark, trying not to think about the ghost pirate ships locals claim to have seen in these waters. The boat was galloping along, the oil lamp above my head swinging wildly. The rigging creaked and groaned, water rushed along the steel hull.

There's no way I'm going to sleep, I thought, but I must have, because suddenly it was 2:00 am, time for my watch.

The wind had definitely picked up, and waves were breaking over the bow, I discovered when I staggered to the head. We'd left the hatch open, and I was treated to a saltwater shower. I grabbed a towel and dried myself off as best I could, then, grumpy and wet, took a little too long to pull on my warm fleecy and boots.

By the time I got above deck, I knew I was in trouble. There's no mistaking that feeling in your stomach. But it was no wonder. While I was sleeping, Chris had been "letting it run," as he calls it. This means carrying way too much sail, going way too fast, and heeling way over as we pound into the waves. He saw the look on my face.

"Let's reduce sail," he said, furling in about half the genoa.

We tied a second reef in the main and the boat slowed down, straightened up a little.

"That's Frying Pan Shoal, off Cape Fear," Chris said, pointing to a light up ahead. "Keep it well to starboard. Oh, and I think there are warships on manoeuvre out here—haven't seen anything, but there's been lots of chatter on the radio. Better keep an eye out."

With that, he gave me a quick kiss and headed below to sleep.

I stood bravely at the helm, watching the approaching light, scanning for ships. No, I told myself firmly, taking big breaths of fresh air and searching for the horizon. But it was pitch black—no moon. And the shore was out of sight. There was no way to orient myself, to straighten out the confused little compass in my head. I could feel my stomach churning as the boat heaved up and down. I checked to make sure the pail was at hand, and, oh my god, okay, here it comes—I heaved what was left of my cheese and crackers into the pail.

I was still retching when an officious voice filled the cockpit.

"To the vessel at…"

I pulled my head out of the pail long enough to check our co-ordinates on the GPS. Of course he was talking to me. I took a couple of brave swallows, reached for the VHF microphone.

"To the vessel hailing, this is the sailboat *MonArk*."

Back to the pail.

"We are an aircraft carrier with limited manoeuvrability. Please maintain a five-mile distance from our position."

I lifted my head from the pail, wiped my chin on my sleeve.

"Roger that."

I had no idea where he was, but I set the radar alarm to six miles and went back to my pail. If anything shows up, I thought, I'll get out of its way.

Thankfully, the radar remained clear, and in time, there was nothing left for me to throw up. I drank some water, threw it up, drank some more, threw it up. It was miserable, but much better than the dry heaves. I looked at my watch — five more hours to go — checked the position of the light, scanned for ships.

It seemed to take forever to come abreast of the light. It was the middle of my watch before it was safely behind us and we were sailing into the dark. No moon. No shoreline. I turned on the radar, scanned for ships. Nothing out there. I checked our position and heading, switched off the instruments. So dark.

I looked down through the companionway. I could just make out Chris wedged into the sea berth with pillows so he didn't fall out as the boat pounded and rocked. He felt me looking at him, opened his eyes, smiled.

"Everything okay?"

"Yep, just fine."

He was asleep again. How does he do that?

I looked back. I could still make out the flashing light marking Frying Pan Shoal, tiny now but still visible.

*What are you doing out here? You don't know what you're doing.*

It's surprising, I thought grimly, how long things take to disappear behind you.

I NEVER WAS much of a farm wife. Not that I didn't try. I helped with the chores — feeding and sweeping were my main responsibilities, I could handle those. Although there was that time I ran over a kitten with the feed cart, which horrified me. Mercifully, the kitten died almost instantly. After that I'd shut all the kittens in the office while I fed the pigs.

I just wasn't ready for the reality of farming, had imagined scattering corn for the chickens on a nice sunny day, helping fill the barn with sweet-smelling hay for the sheep. Chickens, it turns out, are horrible scrappy creatures, will peck a bird to death if it's weak or sick or even just different in some way. When the time came, I took them away to be slaughtered, expected them to come back in neat plastic bags. Bring wash tubs, they told me. I came back home with two zinc tubs full of cold, wet, almost naked birds—I had to pull the pin feathers out before bagging and freezing them. Once. I raised chickens exactly once.

And hay is dusty, I found out. And scratchy. And heavy. At first I tried to help in the mow, carrying bales from where the elevator dropped them to where we wanted to stack them. But I was too slow. The neighbour's wife, who was nine months pregnant, wasn't. She and her husband were helping us, and she matched his pace, bale for bale. Until she decided it was time to go to the hospital, where she very nearly gave birth in the parking lot.

I was relegated to the wagon, to pushing bales down to Brad, who loaded them onto the elevator. Even then, by the end of the day, I was completely exhausted, red in the face and covered with scratches.

But there were worse things. I remember working at the sink one Saturday morning, washing up the breakfast dishes. The screen door creaked open and the vet walked in.

"Let me see your hands."

I pulled them out of the soapy water, held them out for inspection.

"Come with me."

I dried my hands and followed him out to the barn. The sow he'd been called in to help was lying on her side, completely worn out. There were several little piglets nursing, but she wasn't finished giving birth. You could see her straining every few minutes.

"There's a pig inside her that needs to be turned," the vet said. "He's coming out back first. You need to push him back in, turn him, and pull him out head first."

What?

He gave me a long plastic glove that went right up to my armpit, squirted oil all over it. Then he explained how to ease my hand into the sow, slip it past her cervix, push the pig away, and turn him.

"Then grab him by the nose and pull him out."

I didn't really have a choice. I was the only one with small enough wrists to do it. I reached in, farther, farther, until my shoulder was against the sow's hind end and my ear was…well, I tried not to think about where my ear was. There was her cervix. I wormed my hand through and suddenly she had a mighty contraction. Was she going to break my arm? She was trying to push my hand out, I think.

When the contraction subsided, I pushed the piglet away, fished around until I found his nose, then grabbed him behind his milk teeth, as instructed, being careful not to let him bite me, and pulled him out. He was followed by two other piglets and a massive piece of afterbirth. And a lot of blood.

"Good job," the vet said.

Never again, I thought.

But of course I helped with birthing when necessary, and with castrating the pigs when needed. I hated holding the squealing new-borns while Brad made two quick incisions and pulled their tiny testicles out, letting the tendons snap back into place, pretty much sealing themselves. There was almost no blood, but it was still pretty distressing. To me and to the piglets too, I think, though they would just give their little tails a shake and muscle back into their place at their mother's side.

I TRIED TO make a place for myself at the farm, a little room I could call my own. I claimed what used to be the hired man's room — it was wide enough to hold an iron cot and a pair of work boots — papered the bare plaster with cream-coloured wallpaper covered in tiny violets. I found a small maple cabinet in the garage, filled with paint cans, refinished it, and hung it on the wall above my narrow writing table. There was just enough room for a wooden chair. My office,

I called it, a place to do my schoolwork. But more often, I'd find myself looking out at the garden that needed weeding, or the screen door would bang, can you help me for a minute?

I started going missing on my way home from school—it was the only way to keep up with my schoolwork. I'd go to the library, try to get through the 600 pages I had to read by Tuesday, work on the paper that was due Friday. During lambing season, I'd offer to take the night shift, sitting on a bale of hay reading by flashlight long after the lambs that were due that night were safely delivered. One night I was so absorbed in what I was reading that I didn't realize one of the ewes was in trouble. The lamb suffocated before I noticed and was dead when the ewe finally managed to push it out. I was reading *Jude the Obscure*.

Spring came and a sprinkling of snowdrops pushed through the thin crust of ice on the west side of the house. Lily of the valley appeared under the front window, and clumps of grape hyacinth. A carpet of violets spilled out over the lawn.

As the days grew warmer, daffodils came up, and tulips, so many colours. A plant I didn't recognize rose from the damp soil beside the well, all leaves and arching stems, then tiny heart-shaped flowers appeared, pink and white, dangling all in a row. Bleeding heart, my grandmother's favourite flower, according to Mom. I picked a small bouquet, put it in a green fluted vase, placed it on the corner of my writing desk.

One morning in April, it was finally warm enough to let the lambs outside. They hesitated at first, when we opened up the barn door—it was so big outside, so bright. But they followed their mother out into the sunshine and soon they were skidding around the muddy barnyard. Then one of them jumped straight up in the air, just for the fun of it, just because it could.

THE LIGHT MARKING Frying Pan Shoal had disappeared behind me. Blackness all around now. I searched the eastern sky for the slightest bit of light that would tell me dawn was on its way. Nothing.

WE COULDN'T HAVE known interest rates would hit twenty-two percent. There was no way we could make our loan payments, so I dropped down to one night course and we both started working full-time off the farm again. We hired a kid from the village to do the chores morning and night, and we would do all the other things that needed to be done in the evenings and on the weekend. But it wasn't enough.

We held out for as long as we could, falling further and further into debt, then finally gave in and sold the farm to the German who was buying up all the farms in our concession block. We got enough money to pay our debts, almost. We still owed my husband's grandmother more money than we could ever hope to repay, but at least we didn't go bankrupt like so many farmers did in the '80s.

We didn't have much stuff worth moving—a bed, a dresser, a dining room table his grandmother had left behind. We were able to move everything we owned in the back of a pickup truck. It was strange living in the city, locking the door at night, cars going by at all hours. But what bothered me most was not being able to see the sky. You couldn't see what was coming.

NOT THAT I can see much sky right now.

## June 3

~~~~~~

### Day 13

It's been three days since we made the turn and neither of us is getting enough rest — the sound of waves slamming against the hull and the pitching of the boat keep us from falling into a sound sleep. A thousand miles to the Azores. If we can hold 100 miles a day, that's just ten days. I can do it.

But my muscles ache and I'm covered with bruises — I'm getting tired of constantly bracing myself to keep from being thrown into things. I'm not always successful. After two nights of cheese and crackers, I think we're ready for something a little more substantial. A can of soup maybe. I rummage in the locker, come out with a can of Dinty Moore. You know things are bad when a can of stew looks good.

Holding the handrails on the ceiling, waiting for the roll before I take a step, I make my way back to the galley, get a pot out of the cupboard, clamp it to the stove. I set the can in the sink to open it then, wait for the roll, quickly tip it into the pot. There. I light the burner, put the lid on, just as a wave slams against the boat and throws me back against the companionway stairs. I don't care if the stupid stew burns. I climb above deck, sit gloomily in the cockpit rubbing my sore ribs.

"I'll get it," Chris says. "You stay up here."

He's back in five minutes, a tea towel wrapped around the handle of a pot full of steaming stew, two spoons in his other hand. He sets it on the bench between us and we dig in.

"Mmm," he says. "Dinty Moore. So meaty good."

It's still too rough to do anything, so while Chris goes down for his after-dinner nap, I just sit in the cockpit, stare out at the waves. This isn't good. Too much time to think.

WE KEPT A five-gallon pail at the back door of the barn, where Brad would put afterbirth and tiny testicles and little pigs that had been crushed to death by their mother. The dead pail, we called it. Every few days Brad would go out back, dig a hole, and bury its contents. He usually kept a piece of plywood over it, to keep the cats out. But sometimes he would forget to cover it. Don't look, I would warn myself as I walked by. Don't look. Don't look. But I always did. It's hard not to look in the dead pail.

WE WERE AT a cottage we had rented—a new thing since we'd moved to town: summer vacation—when Brad finally decided it was time. His kidneys were failing, we both knew that, but it took him a while to surrender to dialysis. We were both afraid of the next step. We knew exactly what it would do to our lives—at least we thought we did. I had driven my brother John to the dialysis unit at the hospital every second day, watched it take over his life, and in the end, watched it take his life. No wonder Brad was reluctant to make the call.

We had taken the cell phone to the cottage—a good idea, we thought, given the circumstances. I listened to him talking to his doctor as we walked up the road, around a big rock that looked like a bear at dusk. Emily was trotting ahead of us, glancing back from time to time to see what was taking us so long. I had our new puppy, Chester, on a leash.

"Okay," Brad said, listening to the doctor's instructions. "Okay. Friday."

We went back to the cottage and lay down together on the couch in the front of the window overlooking the lake, the dogs curled up on the floor beside us. The three of them fell fast asleep. I didn't. I lay there, looking out at the lake.

We had barbecued ribs for supper that night, his favourite, and corn on the cob and fresh tomatoes from the roadside stand just outside Lakefield. He wasn't very hungry, though, and pushed his plate away before it was clean. As I scraped what was left into the garbage can, I counted the days until Friday.

Just before noon, we stepped off the elevator and into chaos. There were people everywhere, some coming out of the dialysis unit, some going in. We didn't know what to do. We heard Brad being paged but didn't know where to go. A nurse came up to us, recognized me.

"Aren't you John's sister?"

"Yes," I said.

"How is John?"

"He's dead," I said.

I realize now I might have softened it somehow, but it just came out. They paged Brad again.

"That's me," he said.

"Oh, come with me, then. You wait here," she said to me.

Once he was on the machine, she came and got me. Most of the people were in beds. Some of them looked very sick. But he was sitting up in a chair, smiling, as I walked towards him, though he was looking very pale. There were two tubes coming from his chest, just below his collarbone. I felt the room start to swim but managed to collect myself.

"How are you?" I asked.

"Fine," he said. I stood beside him, put my hand on his shoulder.

They didn't keep him on for long that first day, maybe an hour. Afterwards we went to the park. It was an unusually warm fall day, and we just sat on a bench and watched the ducks for a while. Neither of us knew what to say.

I STAND UP, scan through the falling dark for ships. Nothing.

Ten more days. Just ten more days till we make landfall. I can do this.

I DON'T KNOW when it all started going wrong for my brother John. It was sometime in his teens, I think. There was a thin but clear line, in our family, between the big kids and the little kids. Peggy, Brenda, and I were the big kids. John was one of the little kids, even though he was born the same year Brenda was—the babies were coming thick and fast then.

I lost touch with him after I left home. I would get glimpses of him from time to time—I heard that he was working as a welder, knew that he'd bought a muscle car he would drive too fast. He had a girlfriend, then a wife, then a couple of kids. But I was too busy trying to be a good farm wife to take much notice.

Then he started to have some kind of trouble with his heart, couldn't do any heavy lifting, so he had to quit his job. He found work in an electroplating plant, I'm not sure what he was doing, but then he started having episodes of congestive heart failure. This was just the beginning of his troubles.

John had diabetes, which he'd had trouble dealing with, whether because he was a typically invincible teenage boy or because he was actually allergic to the insulin available at that time I don't know. I just knew that in his twenties, his eyesight started to fail, then his kidneys. He had to quit working altogether, stop driving, give up drinking beer with his buddies. His world was getting smaller and smaller.

He needed to live someplace close to the hospital when he started dialysis, so he came and stayed with Brad and me in our first apartment in the city, the one we moved into after we left the farm. He and I would sit up late at night, drinking tea and talking. I was horrified at how ill he was, but he was hopeful about the future. Until he was told that, with his heart condition, he was ineligible for a kidney transplant.

I won't say he gave up after that, but things went downhill pretty quickly. They found gangrene on one of his toes and had to amputate. But that didn't stop it. They took his leg below his knee. Then above. Then the other foot.

There is some debate, in our family, as to which was our worst Christmas ever, but I'd have to say it was the one after John had his second leg amputated just below his knee. He was living at Mom and Dad's by then, and was too ill and in too much pain to come downstairs. I went up to sit with him in his room for a bit, and found him lying on a blanket on the floor, the only place he could stand to be, rocking and crying. I didn't know what to do.

He was in and out of the hospital after that, then they finally admitted him. We all knew he wasn't coming home again. But he hung on for another year, said he didn't want his children to think that giving up was ever an option. But then he did. He decided to stop dialysis, which he knew would end his life. But I don't think he knew how long it would take, or how awful it would be.

Ten days it took, altogether. The fluids built up in his body, and the toxins. We took turns sitting with him, day and night. They gave him something to ease his anxiety, and it did seem to calm him. But it made him hallucinate. One night while I was sitting with him, he said to me, perfectly matter-of-factly, "I know it's not real, but when I look down at the floor, all I see is a big hole. I can see down into the room below us, as clearly as I can see you sitting there." Which was a little disconcerting.

The last night, I was sitting with John when they brought his dinner tray in.

"Will you make my tea?" he asked, not opening his eyes. "Nobody makes it like you do."

This was a kindness he did me when I came to visit. He knew how helpless I felt, how much I wanted to make things better for him. Making his tea was something I could do.

I opened the little metal pot of hot water, dropped the teabag in. When it was just right, I opened two little plastic containers of milk, emptied them into his cup, filled it with tea, stirred it.

"It's too hot," I said. I always said this, even though we both knew the tea was lukewarm at best.

"Better let it cool," he murmured as he drifted back to sleep. I settled back into my chair, opened my book. But he wasn't really asleep.

"Will you read to me?"

"Sure," I said.

So I read to him from a biography of Virginia Woolf while he drifted in and out of consciousness. My brother Dave says that's probably what killed him.

ABOUT A YEAR after John died, I got a call from his heart specialist. I didn't know it, but he had a condition called hypertrophic cardiomyopathy, which causes the heart muscle to thicken and impedes blood flow. This is what had been causing his congestive heart failure. The condition can be hereditary, so he wanted to screen all of John's family members. Reluctantly I agreed to come in. I wasn't sure I wanted to know.

I circled the hospital a couple of times before I parked the car. It was the first time I'd been back since John died, and I really didn't want to go in. But I did, finally. When I reached the clinic, the receptionist looked at her book, frowning.

"Your appointment is next week at this time," she told me.

"Well, I'm not coming back," I said with more force than I intended. She could see I was serious. She went and talked to the technician, who agreed to give up her lunch hour to do my echocardiogram.

I had never seen my heart before, and there it was, flailing around in my chest like a wild thing. I always thought hearts just pumped quietly away, slow and steady. It was hard to imagine that my heart had been working that hard since the day I was born — since before I was born.

"Thank you, little heart," I whispered. "Thank you."

A couple of weeks after my echocardiogram, I received a letter saying I was fine, my heart was normal, but my mother, my sister Sandy, and my brother Dave all had signs of the condition. The family with the thick hearts, I imagined the doctor calling us.

Not thick enough, I wanted to tell him. Not thick enough.

*June 4*

~~~~~~

*Day 14*

And then the wind just dies. By morning the waves have subsided—there's still a ten-foot swell but with a long interval, so it's very gentle, soothing, actually. Up, pause, then down. Up, pause, down. When I come off watch, I sleep for a solid six hours. Six hours! Then Chris goes down for a nap and I fiddle with the sails, trying to make the most of the very light winds.

I go forward to adjust one of the preventers—securely clipped to the jack lines because I'm alone on deck—then stand on the foredeck for a while, just enjoying the sunshine and the fresh breeze. I see a couple of shearwaters in the distance, gliding—okay, shearing—over the water. What are they doing way over there? I wonder idly. They usually follow the boat, waiting for scraps of fish to be thrown overboard. Obviously they can't tell a sailboat from a fishing boat. Then I see a sleek back with a sickle-shaped fin curve slowly out of the water and disappear beneath the surface. A whale!

I'm not sure if I should wake Chris—the whale will be long gone by the time he gets out of bed. I decide to let him sleep, fish my guide to marine mammals out from behind the cockpit cushion. The whale is disappearing in the distance. I can just see it through the binoculars now. It arcs out of the water again. This time I see it blow. A small whale—a minke maybe? So we're not alone out here.

"You missed a whale," I tell Chris when he finally gets up. "I thought about waking you…"

"That's okay. You made the right call. I really needed that sleep."

We have a late breakfast—lunch, really—bacon and eggs, toast, coffee. Our first hot breakfast in a long time. Then I nap for a bit, then he does, stretched out on the cockpit bench with his head on my lap. I read my book, stroke his hair from time to time, keep a lookout for boats. The sails have filled now, and we're sailing steadily over the sparkling sea.

Chris stirs in his sleep, wakes with a smile on his face.

"Want to hear my dream? You and I had a little cottage in the Azores, and we were running a little restaurant. I'd go fishing each morning and you would bake bread. Then at noon, we'd open our restaurant and sell fish sandwiches and wine made from grapes we grew ourselves on our little patch of land.

"In my dream, you were asking a couple of customers if they wanted wine with their lunch. 'I'll have a glass of Pinot Grigio,' the woman said. 'Chardonnay for me, please,' said the man.

"You went to the kitchen and came back with a pitcher of wine.

"'Pinot Grigio for you,' you said, filling the woman's glass.

"'And Chardonnay for you.'"

We both laugh, then he drifts off to sleep again and I go back to lazily scaning the horizon for ships.

*June 6*

〜〜〜〜

*Day 16*

Of course it doesn't last. The wind has picked up again and shifted
to the southwest. Now the waves have thousands of miles to build,
and build they do. We are heading northeast, so we're taking them
on the stern, which is not very comfortable. The wind and the waves
continue to build through the day, and by late afternoon, we're
wallowing along with two reefs in the main and just a little genoa
out—and the stormsail too, in an attempt to keep the boat steady.
But it doesn't work. We continue to wallow sickeningly, except when
two or three waves combine into one big one that sends us slewing
from side to side.

This won't do. Chris keeps trying to raise somebody, anybody on
the SSB to get weather information, but no one responds. We alter
course to the southeast so we're taking the seas on the aft quarter
rather than the stern. The waves are now pounding against the side
of the boat. I'm not sure this is a big improvement.

We eat a cold supper, then Chris goes down for his pre-watch
nap. I decide to make myself a cup of tea—a small enough comfort
as darkness falls. I brace myself against the wall in the galley and put
the kettle on—the stove is gimballed, so it stays more or less level
as we pound along, and the kettle is clamped to the burner, just in
case. While I wait for the water to boil, I get out a cup, pour some
milk into it, put a teabag in. Carefully, carefully, waiting until we
are between waves, I pour the water into the cup, but just then a
big wave slams into us. I watch in despair as a line of milky tea runs

down the front of the counter and across the floor. All I want is a cup
of tea. Is that too much to ask?

I take my half-full cup of tea above deck and carefully, carefully
reach for my iPod. One of the earplugs lands in my cup of tea. That
can't be good. I put it in my pocket to dry and stare gloomily at the
rough, slate-grey sea, covered with whitecaps as far as the eye can see,
except in the distance where it fades into the slate-grey sky.

DIALYSIS IS A blunt instrument, we quickly discovered. Brad would
feel weak but pretty good when he came off the machine. The next
day would be okay, but as the fluids and toxins built up in his body,
he'd feel worse and worse. I don't know what it felt like. I'd look at
him as we drove to the hospital. His face was pretty grim. I think he
was relieved to get there.

We made the best of it, though. We got to be pretty good at
card games, figured out how to lay out the cards on the arms of
his dialysis chair. And when we got tired of that, we found ways to
torment the nurses who in their own way were tormenting him.
One time we tucked a rubber rat into his chart. I don't think the
nurse who found it ever forgave us.

After about a year, he asked me not to come up with him — he
wanted to drive himself there.

"Get on with your life," he said to me. "The best thing you could
do for me would be to just get on with your life."

He'd drive himself to the hospital after work, but couldn't drive
himself home, so around nine o'clock, I'd bike to the hospital, throw
my bike in the trunk of the car, go up to the dialysis unit and collect
him. I'd feel so guilty, walking into the room with cheeks red from
the cold, my hair all windblown, so healthy.

I don't know what he thought getting on with my life would
look like. After he left for the hospital, I'd do the dishes, maybe
take the dogs for a walk. Some nights I'd just lie on the couch in
the dark and hug Emily. Chester would come up and lick my face.
What's wrong? I was afraid I was losing my husband. I was losing
my husband.

It was two years before he had his transplant. During that time, he drifted further and further away from me, moved further and further inside himself. One day I came across a short poem, which I wrote out carefully in my journal.

> *Send me out into another life*
> *lord because this one is growing faint*
> *I do not think it goes all the way*

What if his life didn't go all the way? He hardly had the energy to smile any more. My heart ached for him, but there was nothing I could do. I took care of the house and the dogs as best I could, drove him to the hospital in the middle of the night when necessary. We knew all the nurses in Emergency by the time he had his transplant.

He slept the whole way down to London. It was a beautiful fall day, sunny, cold, the last leaves still clinging to the trees. I kept glancing over at him as he slept. I was afraid. What if this didn't work? We both knew this was his only chance. What if the transplant didn't take? What if he died? I made myself think about it. I'd be fine, of course. I had a good job, the two dogs, our little house in town. My family would take care of me, get me through the really hard part.

But who would remember the time we hitchhiked home from school? I wasn't allowed to hitchhike. I don't know what my mother would have done if she'd found out. But it was easy. Brad just stood beside the highway and stuck out his thumb. The first car that came along was heading for New Hamburg. It dropped us on the highway outside town. The next car that picked us up took us to the Plattsville road. We walked from there. It was raining just a little, and leaves were showering down on us from the big maple trees along the road. My hair was damp, and kept blowing across my face. I'd never felt so free.

If anything happened to him, only I would remember eating meat-loaf sandwiches in the sawdust and concrete forms on our fifth wedding anniversary. The way he would stand in the barnyard shaking the grain pail, calling the sheep in from the pasture, *here, girls, come on, girls*, and they'd come running, follow him into the barn.

THIS LINE OF thinking does nothing to cheer me. I pick up the binoculars, scan halfheartedly for ships. Would I see a ship before it was on us, or would it be hidden by the waves? After a certain point, it's hard to gauge how big they are. All I know is that when we're in a trough, I can't see the horizon at all, which is never a good thing. I switch the radar on. There's no one out here — just us, bounding towards Africa, a place neither of us really wants to go.

Chris doesn't nap for long, and when he comes above deck, he doesn't look like he's slept at all. He checks the sails, adjusts our heading slightly.

"The wind is still clocking," he says. "At this rate, we'll either be pounding into it or heading back where we came from by morning. I'm going to phone Chris Parker."

We haven't used our satellite phone yet. Maybe it's time. He manages to get through on the first try. He listens, nodding his head, looking serious.

"Let's heave to for the night," he says, switching the phone off. "This isn't going to end anytime soon."

We've practised heaving to in heavy weather in the Great Lakes, but this is the first time we've attempted it in seas like these. It's simple, in theory. The goal is to create a balance between the sails and the rudder that stalls the boat at roughly a forty-five-degree angle to the waves. With the bow absorbing the brunt of the waves and the boat in a relatively stable position, you can wait out a storm quite comfortably, in theory. It's getting there that's the challenge.

"This could be tricky," Chris says. "Let's tie another reef in the main and bring the genoa in a little more."

This is not as easy as it sounds. Chris centres the traveller, no simple task with so much force on the mainsail. Then we winch the mainsail down, tie in another reef, and crank in the genoa another couple of feet. When we're done, we have three reefs in the main and just a slip of genoa out — and our handkerchief-sized stormsail.

"Harden up the sheets as much as you can and release the pre-venters," Chris says. With the preventers released, the mainsail will tack on its own when we bring the boat across the wind. Chris waits until we're on top of a wave and turns us hard into the wind.

"Hold on!"

The boat picks up speed and heels over—way over. I'm sitting on the bench on the high side, my feet braced against the lower bench. The rail is buried and water is rushing through the scupper just beneath my feet. It would be easy to lose my footing and slip into the sea. There's no way Chris could turn the boat around and get back to me. I squeeze my eyes shut, clutching the side of the companionway with all my might.

Suddenly the mainsail tacks and the foresails backwind, stalling the boat. Chris adjusts the rudder so we're taking the waves at a comfortable angle on the bow. It's much quieter, no waves pounding against the hull. And we have straightened up (mostly). We're bobbing like a cork as each new wave passes under us. Now we were drifting slowly south rather than racing towards Africa.

Once I'm sure we're settled, I go down and make us tea.

"So Chris Parker can't say how long this will last?" I ask, handing him his cup.

"Not really. A day maybe?"

We sip our tea in silence.

"I'm going to write to Brenda," I say. "You don't mind?"

"Nope," he says, draining his cup. "I'll just have another little lie-down before my watch."

Dear Brenda,

You asked in your last letter how long until we made land-fall in the Azores. I can't really answer that. Since we made the turn, the sailing has been pretty miserable—cold, rough. I can't remember the last time we saw the sun.

A few days ago I would have said ten days. But this afternoon it got so rough we had to alter course away from the Azores. After galloping towards Africa for a few hours, we finally decided to heave to and ride these winds out. We've essentially stalled the boat, nose to the wind and the waves, and it's comfortable enough, bobbing like a cork, but we're not getting any closer to the Azores. We're drifting farther away, in fact. Our distance made good today is exactly zero. We've added at least a day to our journey. Who knows how much distance we'll have to make up by the time we can sail in the right direction again.

It's been too rough to read, Beek, too rough to open my computer, and until now, too rough, even, to make a decent cup of tea. Sadly for you, I have both tea and time to write to you now, before Chris comes up for his evening watch. It's not going to be pretty.

There's just too much time to think out here, Beek. I've been brooding about the farm. I wonder, sometimes, if part of my attraction to Brad was the longing to settle in one place, the family farm, with its generations of continuity.

When we were building sheep pens, I found a wooden box in the old stone shed beside the driveway. In it was a mouldering leather-bound ledger and a bunch of shoemaker's tools — a small hammer, a rusted knife, some wooden-handled awls. Someone must have repaired shoes to supplement the meagre living the farm provided.

There was also a little notebook in the box, with recipes and remedies written out in a spidery scrawl. How to treat a goitre. A cure for cholera. How to make elderberry wine, if all else fails. I could feel the generations that had gone before, was comforted by their presence, somehow.

Did I ever tell you about the night I thought I saw someone in the barn? It was way too late, I was in the old barn, sweeping the aisles. I was bone tired, eyes bleary from lack of sleep. I stopped to straighten my back for a minute, adjusted my dust mask and was leaning on the broom when suddenly the hair on the back of my neck stood up. I wasn't alone, I could feel it.

Cautiously, I looked around, and there, in the doorway to the new barn, was a figure in dusty coveralls, hands in his pocket. I knew right away who it was, recognized him from family photos. It was Uncle Tom, a bachelor who had run the farm with the help of the elderly aunt we had inherited, until one afternoon, between loads of hay, he lay down in the mow and died. They found him stretched out peacefully, hands folded over his stomach.

I wasn't frightened. It felt like he just wanted to help. I think he would have taken the broom from me if he could have. I glanced away for a moment, and when I looked back, he was gone. I could hear Brad at the other end of the new barn, running the pressure washer.

Did I really see that, or did I imagine it? I don't know. The longing to belong somewhere was so powerful. I think you felt it too, didn't you? How could we not? I counted once—by the time I was nineteen, we had moved seventeen times.

But I wonder if that's just how it is, if we all long for a home that never really existed. People remember all the good things about their childhoods, forget the bad. Though in our case there's not that much to feel nostalgic about.

Something else is happening that surprises me, Beek. I'm playing through Brad's slow decline in my mind, remembering every stage of his illness, each more frightening than the one before. I haven't let myself think about it until now. I have to wonder if this is a good time to be reliving it. We both know how it ends. But I don't seem to have a choice. I feel like I'm wandering in a very dark place right now.

So...aren't you glad I can write to you from the middle of the ocean? You always tell me to write about both the good things and the bad. This letter should make up for all the ridiculously happy ones.

I know what to do. I'm going to try to make myself another cup of tea. Chris will be up from his nap soon, and I'm sure a thermos of hot tea will help him get through his watch. He'll have trouble staying awake tonight—we're both so tired. I think it's time for the package of chocolate-covered cookies I have hidden away. That should perk him up.

And I will get my broodiness in hand before I write again,
I promise.

Love you.
Linda

I CLOSE THE lid of the computer, wait for my eyes to adjust to the
darkness, scan the horizon carefully. I can't see any lights, but that
doesn't mean there's nothing out there. I switch on the radar, let it
do a few sweeps. Nothing.

I SLEEP FITFULLY while Chris stands the first night watch. I'm groggy
and grumpy when I come up at midnight.
    "Hey!" I say. Chris is stretched out on the bench. How long has
he been asleep?
    "I've got an alarm set," he says, sitting up hastily. No sleeping on
watch is one of our strict rules. "There's nothing to watch, really."
    He's right. And he's set the radar alarm to alert us if anything
comes within five miles. No sails to tend—the boat's just drifting
with the wind. No point checking our heading. There's nothing we
can do about it.
    But I can't—won't—sleep when I'm on watch. I curl up in the
corner of the cockpit and stare out over the water. There's no moon
at all now, but the sky has cleared a little and by the light of the stars,
I can make out whitecaps in every direction.

THEY WERE READY for us when we arrived at the hospital in London.
A nurse showed us to his room—his theatre, is more like it. The wall
facing the nursing station was all glass, though there were curtains
that could be drawn. Inside there was more medical equipment than
our entire local emergency department had—an entire wall of it,
placed discreetly behind the bed so he wouldn't have to look at it.
    The nurse told him to undress and wait for the doctors, who
were just making their rounds, but he didn't. He wanted to keep his
clothes on for a little while longer. When he finally did take them

off, I wondered, as I hung them neatly in his little locker, when he'd put them on again. If he'd put them on again.

The next morning came too quickly. I was in his room by seven, sat beside him waiting for the gurney to come. When the nurse came and unplugged the machine that regulated the fluid dripping into his arm, he pretended to die. Aren't you supposed to consult the family before you do that? I asked, frowning. We all laughed, but inside I wasn't laughing.

They let me come down to the operating wing with him, let me wait with him in the corridor. He was cold, and I got him a warm blanket. Then they came for him. I kissed him goodbye, and he patted my hand in a distracted kind of way. He was so drugged he could hardly keep his eyes open.

The waiting was the hardest part. I don't know what I would have done if Brenda and Chuck hadn't been there. They took me down to the cafeteria, tried to get me to eat some lunch, but I just couldn't. I can't quite explain what I felt like. Part of me, most of me, was there with him in the operating room. Finally Brenda found a small room for me to wait in, made me lie down on the couch, and stroked my hair while I lay there with my eyes closed.

It was four hours and fifteen minutes before the surgeon came to find me. He was still in his scrubs, or maybe he had put on clean scrubs—there wasn't any blood on them. I couldn't take my eyes off his hands as he talked to me, big, square clumsy looking things. They had been inside Brad. They had held his new kidney.

"It didn't work right away," he said.

What?

"It took about fifteen minutes before the blood started to flow through it."

What?

"But don't worry, in our experience, a slow start has no effect on the final outcome. The new kidney is working fine now."

That's all I wanted to hear. It would be a couple of hours, he told me, before he'd be back in his room.

"Come on," my sister said. "Let's get some fresh air."

Across the road from the hospital is a convent, where the nuns provide rooms for the families of patients. We didn't think they'd mind if we walked around the grounds. We came to a stone grotto carved into the side of a hill, with a statue of a woman in it. The Virgin Mary? Some saint? There were candles tucked in the rocks all around her. I wished that I had one. I wished I knew how to pray.

We found a bench overlooking the river, and sat there, me tucked in tightly between the two of them, feeling their warmth, their strength. Then it was time to go back. I noticed a bush along the path. The leaves were all gone, but little red berries were still hanging on. Hang on, I thought to myself. Hang on. I broke off a tiny branch and put it in my pocket.

HOW LONG UNTIL dawn now? I check the time. Too long. And nothing to do. I pull my iPod out of my pocket. The earbuds don't work.

I scan for blips on the screen—unnecessarily. The alarm would go off if there was anything out there. I check our position. Pretty much exactly where we were before, maybe just a little farther south.

I go back to staring gloomily at the waves.

HE WASN'T BACK yet when I got to his room, so I sat there, in the fading light, watching the late-afternoon sun slant through the blinds onto the bed they'd prepared for him. There were machines all around it, sterile trays on the shelf behind the head of the bed, an oxygen mask ready at hand, other medical equipment I couldn't make sense of—and didn't want to.

I heard the elevator door open, and next thing I knew they were wheeling him in. He was weak and drugged, of course, but he was awake. He didn't see me sitting there. He was surrounded by nurses and orderlies. They transferred him carefully to the bed. He had blood all over him, or maybe it was just iodine.

"Could you step out into the hall for a minute while we clean him up?" a nurse asked me gently.

I stopped and squeezed his hand on the way by.

"Hey there," I said.

He opened his eyes, smiled blearily, tried to squeeze my hand, but fell asleep again before he could.

The next twenty-four hours were critical. I sat quietly in my chair by the window, out of the way of the nurses and doctors, watched the machines blink and beep, watched him sleep.

"Don't be surprised at the colour of his urine," the nurse warned me. "Just a little bit of blood turns it completely red."

And sure enough, the beakers they set beside the sink for the doctors to inspect contained fluid that was more red than yellow. At first, just a few teaspoons each time they emptied the catheter bag, then more, and more. And it became clearer and clearer. The next afternoon, the nurse placed a large beaker of yellow urine on the counter. I think it was the most beautiful thing I'd ever seen.

The morning of the third day, I knew something was very wrong as soon as I walked into the room. He was awake and angry, sweating. There was a cool washcloth on his forehead. I looked over at the counter. No beakers. Just then the doctors came in looking calm but serious.

This is very common, they assured him. You're having a rejection episode. Your body has recognized that the new kidney isn't your own and is trying to isolate it, trying to shut it down. What we have to do is knock out your immune system completely to give it a chance. This isn't going to be fun.

And it wasn't. They gave him a powerful drug that made him throw up until he was so weak he couldn't lift himself up from the bed. He started to run a temperature, started to hallucinate.

"Can you hear that?" he said to me. "Those voices in that vent in the ceiling. I can't make out what they're saying."

The nurse took me aside, asked me if I would stay in his room for the night.

"Sometimes they think we're trying to kill them," she said.

I could understand why.

By morning, he was sleeping quietly. By the afternoon, there were beakers beside the sink again. The worst was over. Or so I thought.

IT MUST BE almost morning—the sky is brightening, if you can call it that. When we're at the top of a wave, I think I can make out a faint line on the horizon between the water and the sky. I scan for ships, sort of, check the radar, nothing. Is it too early to make coffee? Maybe I'll make us a hot breakfast before we start sailing again.

We're both much better after a couple of bowls of steaming oatmeal.

"Ready?" Chris says.

"Just let me stow this stuff." I take the empty bowls and spoons below, stash them in the sink, cushion them with a rolled-up tea towel. I'm not looking forward to getting beaten up again, but the wind is dropping and the seas are starting to calm. And the longer we stay hove to, the farther we drift from the Azores. I put what's left of the coffee in a thermos, double check that I've re-latched all of the cupboards in the galley.

"Okay."

How do you un-heave-to, I wonder. Is it as rough as heaving to?

It isn't. Chris just turns the wheel and the foresails fill with wind. He adjusts the mainsail a little, tightens the sheets, and slowly we pick up speed. We're sailing again. And more or less in the right direction.

By noon, we've made up almost all the ground we lost. Reluctantly, I enter a big fat zero under "distance made good" in the log book. Still 734 miles to go to the Azores.

*June 9*

~~~~~~

*Day 19*

After several more gloomy days the sun comes out, just in time for my first birthday.

I have celebrated two birthdays every year since I was in high school. In order to register for Grade 13, I had to send away for my birth certificate. When I opened the envelope, I was puzzled.

"Mom, why does my birth certificate say I was born June 9th?" I had always celebrated my birthday on June 10th.

"See, George?" my mother said. "I told you she was born on the 9th!"

She mumbled some excuse about having company that weekend. Dad's mother was visiting, I think she said, which always threw my mother into a bit of a state.

I don't remember that particular visit, but I do remember my grandmother, just vaguely. She seemed to me like someone from another century, which I suppose she must have been. She was a plump woman, always wore a dark, flowered dress, tied a white apron over it when she was working in the kitchen. But it's her shoes I remember most, heavy black lace-up things, always polished. She would clomp around the house—Mom's house—with great authority. We were all a little scared of her. And awestruck. Grandma rolled her own cigarettes using a machine. She'd get out her tin of Player's tobacco and her Vogue cigarette papers, which I was allowed to hand her, one by one.

"Careful," my mother would say, when Grandma couldn't hear her. "Don't put your fingers near the cutter."

Grandma would also swear at our dog Tippy, a beagle that never stopped baying.

"Shut up! Damn dog."

"Mother! The children!"

Grandma would switch to Swedish, let out a long string of words that probably meant something much worse than *shut up* and may have been directed at my mother.

So no wonder Mom was a little distracted when she came home from the hospital with me to find Grandma there.

But I wasn't going to let Mom off that easily. She was feeling so bad about the mistake registering my birth that I decided to turn it to my advantage. I announced that from then on I would have two birthdays, and would expect two gifts, two birthday cakes, and most important, two birthday suppers. Mom would make whatever we wanted on our birthday, which made us feel special. I always asked for the same thing: shepherd's pie.

I don't think Mom liked cooking. Or maybe it was just hard, with so many children, so little money. Our likes and dislikes were rarely taken into account. I hated fried baloney with a passion, but it always appeared on the table once or twice a week, the slices curled at the edges, cupping a little pool of orange-coloured grease.

But it wasn't as bad as creamed peas on toast, which she often gave us the day before payday. Or days. I don't know where she got the recipe, if you can call it that. She'd dump a can of peas in a sauce-pan — one can for a family of nine — then thicken the juice with a milk and flour mixture. While it bubbled away, getting thicker and thicker, she'd make the toast. It was all I could do to choke it down.

So that year we had shepherd's pie two nights in a row, though by the time my next birthday rolled around all traces of parental remorse were forgotten. But I still claim two birthdays.

I'm forty-nine today. And tomorrow.

I'm about to go below when the smell of coffee wafts up through the companionway. Clearly Chris is up.

"Hey you. What are you doing up so early?"

"Making your breakfast. Happy birthday!" He climbs up into the cockpit, hands me a cup of steaming coffee and gives me a big kiss. "Your first birthday at sea. Relax. I'll be back in a minute."

I'm dreaming of pineapple turnovers from Antigua, but I know that's not possible. It's our usual cold cereal with milk, but it tastes so much better when someone else makes it.

"Mmm," I say, as we sit beside each other on the cockpit bench, munching our muesli flakes. "This is great. Thanks."

When we're done, he takes our bowls below and refills our coffee cups, then emerges from below with two presents—gifts my sisters sent with us. I had asked him to hide them from me so I wouldn't be tempted to open them before my birthday.

The one from my older sister is clearly a book. But I'm as happy with the card, signed by Peggy and her children, as I am with the gift. I gaze at the familiar handwriting, smile. Then I tear open the package. It's a travel book by Jan Morris, whose writing I greatly admire, a collection of essays about places she has been in the world. I can't stop myself—I flip to the first one and start reading.

"Not yet," Chris says. "There's more."

He hands me the package from Brenda. I take the card off and tuck it into my new book to read later—I know it will make me cry. Then I open the beautifully wrapped box and inside I find little plastic bottles of my favourite facial products. Brenda knows I'm travelling with the bare minimum—waterless cleanser, moisturizer, sunblock, sunblock, and more sunblock. Now I have exfoliant and toner and special eye cream and a foil envelope containing a "refreshing, lifting facial mask." It's a spa visit in a box!

"One more," says Chris.

"What?" These are the only two gifts that came aboard.

He goes below, comes up with a present wrapped in newspaper.

"Forgot to bring giftwrap," he says sheepishly.

How has he hidden this from me? It's a rectangular package about a foot long, six inches wide, a couple of inches thick—not very heavy, so definitely not a book, and anyway, it's the wrong shape. I tear it open — it's a print of a barracuda I had admired at a little shop in Antigua.

"Nowhere to put it," I'd said wistfully. He must have gone back when I was busy doing something.

"Above the fridge in the galley," he says. "I measured it. It will fit perfectly. Look — Velcro on the back so it stays put."

"This is the best birthday ever," I say, giving him a big hug.

"It's not over yet."

AROUND MIDMORNING, THE satphone rings. It takes Chris and me a minute to figure out what is making that sound and then another minute to find the phone. This is the first call we've received.

"Happy first birthday!" It's Brenda. I'm so happy to hear her voice. It's thirty-one degrees in Canada, hot and sunny, she tells me.

"What's it like where you are?"

"It's fifteen here, not hot, not sunny, but the sailing is fine." I don't add, for the moment, though I think it.

"We're back on track. The winds are from the west, which is perfect for us, and the waves are about two feet high with a long interval between them, so it's very comfortable. We're sailing along with the main and genoa fully out, making about six knots. It doesn't get much better than this."

"Sounds like things are going better than they were a couple days ago."

"Yes, much better. I'm sorry about the gloomy letter, Beek."

"Don't be sorry. I want it all, the good and the bad."

"Hey, I had an interesting dream about you last night. You were sitting in front of a mirror and Peggy was standing behind you, arranging flowers in your hair. Clearly you were getting married and she was the maid of honour. I looked across the room and there were Sandy and Jenn.

"'What!' I cried. 'You're bridesmaids too?' I started crying and ran from the room. You followed, trying to placate me, but I was so angry and hurt. I woke with tears on my cheeks."

"Hmm, I guess we don't have to look at that very deeply," she says.

"I miss you, Beek. Sometimes I think about all the things I left behind. I was in such a hurry to get away."

"Maybe I'll come see you in the fall," she says. "Anna did fine when Chuck and I went away for a week. Let me work on it."

Then she puts Anna on the phone. It's such a joy to hear her little voice. She tells me that she has some new barrettes, and that the Funky Mamas are coming to her daycare. I hear Brenda in the background.

"Thank you for the Nemo purse," she says. Then, "I love you."

"Did you tell her to say that?" I ask Brenda when she comes back on the line.

"No, she came up with that on her own."

Maybe she hasn't forgotten me after all.

I ask Brenda if she's thinking of joining the Funky Mamas, and she laughs, tells me about her busy life — the psychology clinic is going through some growing pains, she's been asked to do a television documentary on death and dying, she's renovating her kitchen. And of course there's Anna, who is herself a full-time job.

"How's Mom doing?" I ask her.

"Amazingly well. I took her to a tea party on Sunday, women only. She was waiting for me in the lobby with a big, floppy red hat on her head, wearing bright red lipstick. When I wheeled her into the party room, she was all smiles, greeting people right and left. This is the same woman who wouldn't leave the house without Dad. I wonder, sometimes, if the stroke broke her open somehow, in a good way. She seems so much happier, just laughs when she slops tea in her saucer or drops cake in her lap."

"I miss her," I say. "It's hard to stay in touch with someone who can't speak. But believe me, I still hear her voice — Oh my god, look at those clouds! Get below. Is this safe? What are you doing way out here? What if one of you gets hurt?"

We both laugh. There is so much more I want to say, but I must let her go. The phone call is costing her a fortune.

"Thanks for calling, Beek. I love you."

AFTER LUNCH, CHRIS goes down for a nap—at least that's what I think he's doing. I read Brenda's card and have a good cry, then I heat up some water and grab a fresh towel—it's spa time. I stretch out on the back deck while the mask cures. Yes, I know it's wrong to bask in the sun, but it's my birthday. When I'm finished, I settle in the cockpit with my new book. This is nice. Hmm. I can smell something baking.

Around four, Chris emerges from below, fully washed and cleanly shaven, dressed in the soft white chambray shirt I love and a pair of jeans. He hands me a glass of wine. I raise an eyebrow.

"It's your birthday," he says.

We never drink while on a passage, but surely one glass of cold Chablis will do us no harm. I try to sip mine slowly, but it just tastes so good. Chris produces a small round of Brie and cuts me a slice.

"Where did you get this?" I ask, trying not to wolf it down.

"Canned Brie," he says. "I found it in Antigua. Not bad, eh?"

"Where have you been hiding it?"

He just smiles.

"Relax. Enjoy your wine. Dinner will be ready in ten minutes."

Next time he comes up, he's carrying two plates of spicy peanut chicken on a bed of rice.

"Even better than Dinty Moore," I say as I clean my plate. It's delicious. "Is there more?"

"Yes, but you need to leave room for dessert."

He disappears below again, and I smell coffee brewing. He hands two steaming cups up through the companionway, then two plates with slices of fresh-baked birthday cake, icing and all.

We end the day in much the same way we started it, snuggled in on the bench, sipping coffee. It takes forever for the light to fade, which is fine with me. Then the sun slowly disappears into the sea behind us.

Thank you hardly seems like enough.

This has been my first birthday without my family, I think, as I settle in for my night watch. Well, some family, anyway. I haven't seen my younger sisters Sandy and Jenn in years. They moved out west many years ago and haven't been home since. My brother Dave lives in Hamilton, an hour's drive from Waterloo, but he might as well live in Antarctica, our worlds are so far apart. Peggy and Brenda have always celebrated my birthday with me, and Peggy's daughters, Kathy and Kim. I miss their faces.

I scan for ships, then as quietly as I can, I creep down the companionway, rummage in my drawers until I find the small leather photo album I've brought with me. I settle back into the cockpit, switch on a flashlight, open the album.

There's Peggy, sitting at the table at the farm. She has stopped by for tea and Scrabble, on her way back from the feed mill. She's holding a tiny raccoon on her lap, Coonie, I called him. Very imaginative. I found him in our woodshed, abandoned by his mother, I guess, was raising him in the house. But he was a wild little thing. Peggy is laughing, her face turned away, as Coonie lunges for her throat. Her long, dark hair is tied back from her face with a red bandana. This is my favourite picture of her. She looks so tanned, so happy. Clearly the picture was taken before the recession hit.

Flip. There's her daughter Kathy, standing in front of the sink at the farm. She's about eight, I think. It's a close-up of her, and you can just see the African violets on the windowsill behind her. Her short brown hair frames her face, her dark green eyes look directly into the camera. She's smiling defiantly. Oh, yeah? Just watch me.

And there's her little sister Kim, squatting in the sun porch. I remember that linoleum, something Brad's grandmother chose, an ugly green and orange and yellow pattern. I hated it. It was worn smooth in front of the door, and the seam in the middle of the room was starting to lift. No matter how much I scrubbed it, it never looked clean.

Kim looks up at the camera warily, she's brought a cat in from the barn, she knows they're not supposed to come in the house. But she loves this cat, a mangy-looking orange thing we called Mama—I'd lost track of how many litters of kittens she'd had. Kim is hugging the cat to her chest. The cat is struggling to get away, its ears back. I can't remember how that scene ended.

Brenda. There's Brenda. Was she ever that young? She's in the sheep barn, wearing her work clothes — a pair of rubber boots, jeans, a red plaid shirt. She's helping us with the chores, bottle feeding a lamb in the straw at her feet. Her black shoulder-length hair is held back from her face with a couple of barrettes. I study her face, so smooth, so soft. She's smiling gently at the little creature, which can't be more than a few days old. Mama is rubbing against Brenda's legs, can I have some milk? Is there any left for me?

There are pictures of my little dog Emily, and of Chester, but no pictures of my parents. The pictures of Mom since she had her stroke are too heartbreaking to look at — she looks so confused, and sad. It didn't seem right to bring an earlier picture, she's a different person now. And anyway, I won't forget what she looks like.

The last time I saw Mom, she was sitting in her room at the nursing home, smiling bravely but wiping away tears. I'm not sure if she was crying because the hairdresser had done such a brutal job on her hair, cut it short and permed it tightly, or because I was leaving. Maybe both. Or maybe she was crying because Dad was going to join us for the first part of our trip down the Erie Canal. He hadn't spent a night away from her since she had her stroke.

I DON'T THINK I've ever seen Dad as excited as he was the day Brenda dropped him off at the boatyard in North Tonawanda. He started talking the moment he stepped out of the car and didn't stop until he went to bed that night. (He may still have been talking, but we couldn't hear him from the aft cabin.) I wasn't sure he'd be able to climb from the rickety floating dock onto the boat, a distance of two or three feet. But he just handed Chris his cane and heaved himself up.

"That wooden structure back there is the remains of an old swing bridge," Dad began as we cast off.

Though there wasn't much room to manoeuvre in the narrow channel, Chris steered the boat around the structure so Dad could have a good look at it. Dad was explaining the mechanical workings of swing bridges (to Chris, a mechanical engineer) as we circled, but we were more focussed on the modern bridge up ahead. With our mast down, we were sure we'd have no trouble clearing it—we'd measured and remeasured the night before—but we held our breath as we passed beneath it. Even Dad stopped talking for a moment. We cleared the bridge just fine, traffic roaring overhead, water dripping down on us, and passed under the next four bridges in rapid succession. Before we knew it, we were out of the city.

"There are several ways to get to the ocean," Dad began once the bridges were behind us. "I've studied the maps carefully. You can get there by going down the St. Lawrence or the Mississippi, but this is the shortest way, down the Erie Canal to the Hudson River, then into the ocean at New York City."

Chris looked at me as Dad launched into a discussion of the pros and cons of each of the routes. We both knew that he would come all the way across the ocean with us if he could. But Mom was probably already sitting in her wheelchair by the front door—I think she loses track of the days sometimes—watching every car that pulled up, waiting for him to return to her safe and sound, and with some new stories.

Much of the Erie Canal isn't actually canal—you travel along creeks and rivers, and across small lakes. For the first couple of hours, we followed the winding Tonawanda Creek. Then we left the creek and entered a long stretch of dug canal. As the waterway widened and straightened out, the overhanging bushes on either bank gave way to open farmland.

I asked Dad if he wanted to take the helm, told him the boat steers just like a car. Okay, it's not quite as easy as that. The boat weighs twenty tons and has a six-foot lead keel. It takes a bit more time to respond than a car does, which makes it easy to overcorrect. In no time, Dad had us heading straight for one of the stone banks.

"Back to the left, Dad. Just easy."

He eased the wheel to the left, then when there was no response, turned it a little more. Suddenly we were heading for the other wall.

"Back to the right, Dad, but just a bit."

He cranked it to the right.

"No, that's too much. Ease it back a little."

Flustered, he turned the wheel even more to the right.

"Here, let me take it for a minute."

I straightened the boat out, and once we were on a steady course again, I gave him back the wheel. This time I issued a steady stream of directions: "A little to the left. No that's too much, back a bit. Now to the right. That's good there. Just wait, it will come back."

Before long, he got the hang of it, but I was taken aback at how long it took him. I was also secretly pleased that there was something I could do that he couldn't, that I had taught *him* something. I was certainly more patient than he was when he was teaching me to drive. I remember him shouting at me as I just about hit a cyclist coming up the hill by the hospital. Which would have been a good place to do it.

We made it as far as Lockport that first day. Dad wanted to take us out for dinner, but it was cold and rainy, and we couldn't find a restaurant. Many of the stores in the downtown area were boarded up, and the ones that weren't were closed, except for the pawn shop and the discount bridal store. We decided to eat on board.

Chris was worried about Dad getting cold, so he worked away at starting the diesel furnace, which we hadn't used in a couple of years, while I put supper on.

"This," I said, as I set Dad's plate down in front of him, "is the official gorp of *MonArk*. A can of mushroom soup, a handful of rice, a can of tuna, and a can of green beans."

It actually tastes a lot better than it sounds, and in no time, we'd cleaned our plates and were sprawled comfortably around the cabin, mugs of coffee in hand. Above our heads, the rain beat against the deck and the wind rocked the boat gently, making the oil lantern swing from side to side. But we were warm and dry.

"My dad used to make gorp," Dad began, putting his feet up.

I knew we were in for a long one, but I listened with interest. I didn't know his father ever cooked. In all the stories I'd heard, he was either off trying to find work or sitting at the kitchen table with a bottle in front of him. But it turns out that he and Dad spent a couple of summers together at Wasaga Beach building cottages.

Grandpa had built a wooden platform and pitched a tent on it, and that's where the two of them lived for the summer. They had a little stove in the tent, and when they came home at the end of the day, Grandpa would heat up some gorp.

"He'd put whatever food we had into the pot. One night he put half a jar of pickled beets in. I don't know why he did that. We both hated beets, but Mom had sent them along, and he couldn't stand to see food go to waste. She knew we both hated beets."

Dad didn't offer to take the helm on the second day. He made himself comfortable on the bench in the cockpit and assumed the duties of navigator. But more than once he got confused about where we were.

"We'll be coming up on a bridge around the next bend," he'd say, but there would be nothing there. We had passed that bridge fifteen minutes ago. Chris and I took to checking the charts when Dad wasn't looking.

It was a long day, but by evening we made it to Fairport, just outside Rochester, where Dad would catch his train in the morning. I think being in the canal made him think about my brother John. Towards the end, Dad used to take him to the Welland Canal whenever he could. He'd tell Mom he was taking John to a doctor's appointment or out to get groceries, but the two of them would always end up at their favourite spot just below one of the locks. (Mom didn't like it when they went there. Not safe. Dad could stumble and fall in. John could roll over the edge.) They'd sip their coffee and wait for a boat to come through. When Dad saw the lock opening, he'd edge John's wheelchair to the side of the canal and John would lean forward and put his hand out to feel the rush of air as the wall of steel passed by him.

While I cleared away the plates and made a pot of coffee, he started telling Chris about the time he and John went sailing in Hamilton Harbour. Oh, this is a good one, I thought.

John had arranged the whole thing with the help of the social worker at the hospital. The first challenge was getting John on board. While Dad and the captain tried to figure out some way to rig a bosun's chair,

John wheeled his chair as close to the boat as he could get, grabbed the gunwales, and heaved himself over the side. John was pretty tall, and without legs, a little top-heavy. He teetered on the gunwales for a minute, then landed on the cockpit floor with a heavy thud.

"I meant to do that," he said with a grin, pulling himself up onto the bench.

Once they were clear of the docks, the captain handed John the tiller and told him to aim for the bridge, then went forward to raise the sails. He didn't know that John was almost blind. Before long, the boat was veering towards the breakwall. The captain didn't blink an eye.

"More to starboard," he said calmly.

John eased the boat to the left.

"The other starboard."

John eased the boat to the right, and the sails caught the wind.

"Now just keep the sails full."

That was something John could do. He could feel the wind on his face, feel the boat surge ahead when he got it right. I can just see the two of them — the boat racing across the harbour, Dad hanging onto his Tilley hat, John at the helm, one hand on the tiller, the other resting casually on the back of the bench, sun on his face, wind ruffling his hair, mirrored sunglasses hiding the fact that he can't really see where he's going. I think it's as close to free as he ever got. As either of them ever got.

I couldn't help thinking of the two of them when the gates swung open and we motored out of the last lock in the Erie Canal. There was nothing between us and the ocean but a long stretch of river. As I stood at the bow, coiling our docklines, I found myself scanning the side of the canal. I knew they weren't there, but in my mind I could see them, watching me, Dad with one hand on the back of John's chair, John peering in the wrong direction. Dad raises his arm, waves his hat, and I wave back, with a heavy heart.

Sometimes the weight of being the one who got away is almost unbearable.

*June 10*

~~~~~~

*Day 20*

That's pretty much the last we see of the sun. The morning of my second birthday dawns overcast and cool, but the sailing is still good. I spot a big container ship on the horizon, keep my eye on it as it approaches. They're unwieldy-looking things when they're fully loaded. We saw them at anchor in the outer harbour at New York City, waiting their turn to unload. At sea they're even more ungainly, but pretty from a distance, with their stacks of multicoloured containers. They look like toy boats carrying Lego. Until they get closer.

I watch nervously. It's really moving, but clearly it's seen us. It's going to pass well off our bow.

"Are you sleeping, little sailboat?"

I jump. The radio has been silent for days, weeks maybe. And I'm not sure what to say. We've never been hailed by a commercial ship, at least not in a friendly sort of way. I assure the captain that I'm awake, and he asks me where we're headed. I say the Azores, and he tells me it's one of his favourite places, though he seldom stops there. He's hauling cargo from the Med to New York City; he comes from Albany himself.

"Cataplana," he says. "You gotta try cataplana." He describes it in great detail — rice, prawns, clams, and spicy sausage, cooked with tomatoes and lots of paprika. Sounds like he's tired of ship's rations.

"And those little custard tarts." He can't remember what they're called, but they have crisp, flaky pastry and a sweet, creamy filling.

My mouth is watering. I want a custard tart for breakfast.

I assure him we will try both. We chat for a while longer, then say goodbye before he's out of radio range. I watch the ship disappear over the horizon. At that speed, he'll be in New York long before we reach the Azores.

There's been a heavy dew, so I take the opportunity to wipe the salt off the windows with a towel, then I clean them properly for the first time since we left Antigua. When I'm done, we can actually see out of them — we don't have to unzip the plastic to scan for ships. Might as well clean the hatches and portholes too, while I'm at it. I have to sneak down to wipe the insides of them, which I do as quietly as possible so I don't wake Chris. By the time I'm done, all the windows sparkle — as much as they can on such a grey day.

I think of getting myself a pail of seawater and going forward to scrub the bottom of the dinghy, which still has gunge on it from our long stay in English Harbour in Antigua, but I'm beat. We're both working through a haze of fatigue these days, which is dangerous. We've sworn to start sticking strictly to our watch schedule, so when Chris gets up at 8:00 am (oops! I was supposed to wake him at 6:00), we have a quick bowl of cereal together before I go down for my morning nap.

When I get up at noon, I make us toast and peanut butter (this qualifies as a hot lunch when I just don't feel like cooking). Then Chris goes down for his afternoon nap, and I make myself comfortable in the cockpit with a cup of tea and my new book. Before long I have to close up. A band of light showers is passing over us. If April showers bring May flowers, what do June showers bring?

The snowdrops and tulips and daffodils will be done by now, but the bleeding heart around the well at the farm might still be out, rows of deep pink hearts with a little white tear falling from each one, and the lily of the valley, and the grape hyacinth. I don't think there's anything prettier than a bouquet of bleeding heart, lily of the valley, and grape hyacinth, in that low, green fluted glass vase that was my grandmother's. Where did that go?

For sure the lilacs will be starting, light purple ones beside the rhubarb patch, white ones on the north side of the wood shed, pale purple-blue ones towering over the greenhouse, deep purple ones on the other side of the laneway. But best of all, the lacy purple ones beside the sheep barn—French lilacs, Brad's grandmother called them. I used to pick great bunches of lilacs, put them in jars in the middle of the kitchen table, on my dresser, on my writing table.

It won't be long now until the irises and peonies below the kitchen window begin to bloom. I forget which peonies open first—the pink ones, I think—but soon they will all be out: the white ones, the red ones, the white ones with red streaks. I liked to put peonies and irises together in a jar. The irises would stand so stiff and proper, bloom slowly, last a long time, while the peonies, tight little balls at first, would burst into flower quickly, then scatter their petals on the table. I wonder sometimes which way is better.

There will be flowers in the Azores, I remind myself. We're planning to make landfall on Flores—I'm sure it's called the Isle of Flowers for a reason.

The rain has stopped and it's getting a little brighter. I unzip the side panels, go back to my book. Then I hear a splash behind the boat. I get up and look.

"Chris!" I shout. "There's something big under the boat!"

He's up in an instant. "What?"

I tell him that I heard a splash, saw a big swirl in the water just off our stern. He looks skeptical, is about to go back down, I think, when a killer whale surfaces beside us, not six feet away from the boat.

I should be scared, I guess. I'm sure they're called killer whales for a reason. But it's just beautiful, its dark back glistening as it breaks the water, a flash of white before it dives again. It has a funny fin on its back, maybe two feet tall, that stands straight up. Wait, not it—she! Next time the whale breaks the surface, there is a calf beside her. They swim beside us for a good half hour, the mother always careful to keep herself between her calf and us. She tips her head sometimes as she surfaces beside us, watching us with one dark eye. She has a stark white chin, and a white patch just above her eye, in sharp contrast to her jet black back. I wish Brenda could see this. Then they disappear as suddenly as they arrived.

"Okay, that was a great second birthday present," I say.

The show's over, but we sit on the cabin house for a while, watching the sails breathe in and out. The wind has dropped and the seas are as smooth as glass now, and an impossibly dark blue. We're in the deepest part of the North Atlantic, over 10,000 feet, though we have to take the chart's word for it: the depth sounder stopped registering a long time ago. I think of what they say on Jack's ship when they can't get a sounding: No bottom with this line.

"Better check the weather," Chris says at last.

We're reluctant to go back to the cockpit, but we do. I check our course, adjust the sheets a little to try to make better use of what little wind there is, and Chris goes below.

"A mild frontline is going to pass over us in the next day or two," he says, "but nothing we can't handle."

*June 11*

~~~~~~

*Day 21*

The good sailing doesn't last. It never does. The next day, the winds die altogether and before long, we're motoring over flat seas. By noon, we have just 549 miles to go, five and a half days, if we can hold this course and speed. Five and a half days.

We spend the afternoon doing chores—Chris empties a jerrycan of diesel fuel into the starboard tank, and I tackle several days' worth of dishes. As I fill the sink, I hear the water pump whine—we've emptied our first water tank, not bad after two weeks at sea. I switch to the other tank, take a quick look in the V-berth. Yep, still lots of four-litre jugs of water left, and we haven't touched any of the twenty-litre jugs lashed along the deck. We're fine.

When I've finished the dishes, I fill the stove, straighten the sea berth, and just generally put the cabin back in order. But I'm keeping an eye on the barometer, which is dropping fast.

Chris is above deck, seeing what he can do about the mainsheet becket, which let go in the night and set the boom loose, taking out the SSB antenna before we could secure it.

"I have good news and bad news. I can't fix the becket," Chris reports. "But I've rigged something up that will do for now."

That's the good news. What's the bad?

"The SSB antenna is beyond repair. It wasn't really working anyway."

Somehow this does little to reassure me. No more weather information. No more email. We're really on our own now.

We've been at sea for twenty-one days now. Three weeks. That's how long it took my great-grandmother to make the crossing from Sweden. In 1880. If she could do it, travelling in steerage, in the bottom of a ship that had once hauled cattle, surely I can.

She was interviewed when she was 104, talked a lot about the crossing. There were many, many people in steerage, men, women, and children all huddled together. There were beds of a sort for families, but single people slept in hammocks. The toilets were up one deck—they wouldn't work below the water line. She was allowed to go up there in the daytime to use the toilet and to play sometimes. But I doubt she ever got above deck.

All she could see through the portholes in steerage was water. In heavy weather, she would watch warily, hoping the glass wouldn't break. It didn't. But they would get wet anyway—water would splash down through the fresh-air vents above their heads, soaking them and their belongings.

She never got seasick, but most of the others did, including her mother, who was pregnant at the time. She wasn't the only one—nine babies were born at sea.

If the sea didn't make you sick, my great-grandmother said, surely the food would. Great troughs of oatmeal were sent down to steerage for breakfast. For dinner, undercooked meat and hard bread were provided. Not surprisingly, many people died on the crossing and were buried at sea. I'm not sure the food didn't do some of them in.

I have a picture of my great-grandmother, a determined-looking woman in wire-rimmed glasses, short, curly grey hair combed back from her broad face. She's smiling, almost, and there is a glint in her eye, as though she is about to say something you wouldn't expect to hear from an elderly woman. Did the crossing shape her in some way, I wonder? Or is that just how she was. Bold, like my grandmother. I'd never thought about that. Maybe I come from a long line of strong women on my father's side.

The winds pick up in the night, catching us with too much sail up. We tie three reefs in the main and put out just a slip of genoa to balance us, but it's still very rolly. Clearly there's some weather moving in. The temperature and the barometer continue to drop. We're both too tired for this. Like we have any choice.

*June 12*

~~~~~~

*Day 22*

By noon the next day, we have 360 miles to go. Three days, if all goes well. The seas have definitely picked up. I scan the water around the boat, trying to gauge the height of the waves. There's a small bird — what's he doing so far from shore? — skimming above the water in the trough between two waves. Must be a storm petrel — they migrate far out to sea. Sailors say a storm petrel means rough weather.

Shortly after the incident with the shotgun, my grandma and grandpa loaded their five children and a dog into a Model T touring sedan, hitched a box trailer piled high with their belongings to the back of it, and set out on the long drive from California to his parents' farm near Washington, Ontario. A few of the roads they travelled were paved but most were gravel and some were just dirt tracks. Occasionally they would find a campground or a cabin, but most of the time they just spread their mattresses out on the ground and slept under the open sky.

I still don't know what they were running from. My dad wasn't born when this happened, and his brothers and sisters don't like to talk about it. But clearly they were running away from something.

What are we doing, I wonder, as I look out over the slate-grey seas.

Just after lunch the wind dies suddenly and the temperature plummets. We get out our foul-weather gear, stow for the worst, spend the afternoon taking turns sleeping as much as we can. The seas calm enough for me to make us a hot supper, nothing elaborate, just some soup and crackers, which we eat in silence. I think we're both a little nervous about the weather. I know I am.

The night sky is completely overcast, it has never been so dark, or at least that's how it seems to me. I scan for signs of a storm, but I can't see anything. So I stand at the helm, hands on the wheel (even though we're on autopilot), ready for whatever comes up.

But I'm not ready for the dark thoughts that come crowding in.

DAD NEVER COULD really settle at anything—he was always looking for better ways to feed his growing family, but I think the truth is he just got restless. He moved from one job to another, even if it meant uprooting us and moving to another province. Mom always followed, made the best she could of each new situation.

Once when we were between houses, Dad arranged for us to stay at a cabin in the Laurentian hills north of Quebec City for the summer. He would drive to his job in the city each day, leaving Mom and three small children—she was pregnant with her fourth—in a rundown shack, really, clinging to the side of a hill. We looked down over a long field to the road, cultivated once, perhaps, but now just scrubby bushes. The occasional deer would wander through, and we were always on the lookout for bears. Mom wouldn't let us play beyond the small cleared area around the cabin.

There was running water in the kitchen, and there must have been an indoor toilet of some sort, but there were no bathing facilities, so once a week Mom would set a big washtub out in the yard and fill it with water. We'd take turns bathing, smallest to largest, or dirtiest to cleanest, as the case may be.

One afternoon, I was splashing in the tub and Mom was sitting on a lawnchair beside me, eyeing the bush, when I spotted a little striped snake under her chair.

"Look, Mom," I said. "There's a snake under your chair."

She was up and in the house in no time, door slammed shut behind her. I don't know what kind of snake she thought it might be, but I do remember wondering why Mom left me outside alone with it, if it was so dangerous. I'd seen nature shows on TV, I knew that mother animals were supposed to protect their young. I sat there, watching the tiny snake watch me, its pink tongue darting in and out, until it quietly slithered away.

When I was thirteen, Dad decided that he wanted to return to the part of rural Ontario where he was born, so he bought a small general store, just like the one his father had owned. We packed up all our things and left our comfortable apartment in Montreal to move to the tiny village of Washington in southwestern Ontario.

The old insulbrick house that came with the store had two bedrooms (for our family of eight — there were six children by then), running water only in the kitchen, and no proper toilet. Mom and Dad slept in the dining room, one tiny bedroom was assigned to the girls, the other to the boys, which didn't seem fair to me — there were four girls and only two boys. I complained bitterly about this and was allowed to sleep in the tiny pantry off the kitchen, which had just enough room for a rollaway cot. The room didn't have a door, so I put a thick curtain across the doorway.

The lack of proper plumbing was the biggest problem. Mom would set up a square zinc tub in the kitchen on Saturday nights, fill it with water, and we'd take turns bathing. But I was fierce about my privacy, so I'd fold up my cot and drag the tub into my little room, yank the curtain shut.

But there was no way to avoid the embarrassment of the chemical toilet, which was actually just a five-gallon pail with a plywood seat over it in a lean-to off the kitchen. Every night, after dark, Dad would haul it to the septic tank in the backyard and empty it. By which time the pail was pretty full.

I'll never forget the day I started my period. I was distressed at the blood in the toilet, but not as distressed as my brother was when he used the toilet after me.

Once Mom had calmed him down, she gave me a strange-looking belt and a box of pads and warned me that I was to stay away from boys now. I didn't know what that meant. My brothers? The boys on the school bus? The kids at school? What if a boy came into the store — what was I supposed to do?

The store went bankrupt, of course. You can't feed a family of eight by selling milk and bread, especially when the only factory in town shuts down. So things went from bad to worse. We had to move out of the house, ended up renting a farmhouse on a back road. Mom never complained, but I'm sure she wondered what she'd gotten herself into.

Black. It's still completely black outside. I can't see a thing.

On my good days—most days—I feel like I'm free, like I've run away. On my bad days, I worry that I'm just like my mom, that I'm just following the first man who came into my life, one I found (quite literally) sitting on my back step, that I'm trailing after him while he chases his dream.

*June 13*

~~~~~~

*Day 23*

At noon the next day, I mark our position on the chart. Just 247 miles to go. At this rate, we'll make landfall at Flores in two days. In the middle of the night, actually. It's a tricky harbour, so we'll have to stand off, wait until it gets light to enter. Then we'll drop the anchor and sleep, together, for the first time since we left Antigua.

Chris has just gone down for his after-supper nap when a sailboat appears on the horizon. A woman hails us, in French. When I respond in my very best French, she switches to English. They are seventeen days out of Guadeloupe, heading for Brittany.

"A minute," she says. "Sorry. I get my daughter some juice."

They are sailing with two children, a girl who is five and a son who has just turned four. I ask her for weather information. There's a mild front coming through, she says, but nothing to worry about. I am somewhat, but not entirely, reassured. She thinks sailing across an ocean with two kids is nothing to worry about.

"Oh, my son is waking. I must go and kiss and love him," she says. "*A bientôt.*"

My conversation has wakened Chris. He, too, is concerned about the "mild front."

"I'm going to put a call in to Chris Parker," he says.

Thank goodness for the satphone.

Minutes later he comes above deck, looking grim.

"There's a big front coming through overnight, but he says the worst of it should pass north of us. We should reduce sail just in case."

We tie in a reef, two reefs. Just in case. We're motoring anyway. Still no wind.

Hold on tight, I think. That's all you've got to do.

# CLOBBERED

*June 14*

~~~~~

*Day 24*

Of course it happens on my watch.

We know it's coming because the seas have been building steadily. It's a pitch-black night, no moon, and anyway, the sky is completely overcast. Around 2:30 the wind picks up sharply. Chris comes above deck and helps me tie a third reef in the main, we furl in the genoa just enough to keep the boat balanced, then he goes back down, even though I know he will not sleep. I stand at the helm, peering into the darkness. The autopilot has it for now, but I'm ready. Or so I think.

Suddenly we are hit by a blast of wind—where is it coming from? I lean forward to check the windvane at the top of the mast. Without thinking I clutch the top of the autopilot display to steady myself and inadvertently push the "dodge" button, which puts control of the helm in my hands. But I don't know this, and I'm not holding the wheel, so the boat is at the mercy of the wind. We jibe with such force that the preventers, which secure the boom to the deck, are ripped out of the boom as it slams from one side of the boat to the other. The genoa and stormsail backwind, stopping our forward motion, but we're heeled over way too far, the starboard rail disappears in the foaming water as each wave hits us.

In a flash, Chris is in the cockpit.

"What happened?"

"The boat hove to," I say, not willing to admit my part in the calamity.

"Let's not argue with it. But we need to get ourselves straightened up."

*Why don't you tell him what happened? Your fear got the best of you. You panicked.*

The voice in my head is almost drowned out by the shrieking of the wind.

Inch by painful inch, he cranks in the genoa until just a slip remains. Slowly the starboard rail emerges from the water. Next we try to centre the mainsail, but in these winds it's almost impossible. We do the best we can, but without the preventers, there's no real way to secure the boom, so Chris tightens the main sheet, lashes down the boom as best he can from the cockpit. Then he adjusts the rudder, half a turn this way, back a little, back a little more, until the bow is taking the brunt of the waves.

"There," he says. "That's the best we can do."

It's not very good. It is just starting to get light and we can see that the mainsail is full of little bellies. But it's not safe to go forward with the boat pitching and rolling so wildly. So we sit in the cockpit, watch the mainsail flog and shudder, watch the preventers dangling in the wind, listen to the wind howling through the rigging. The seas are a mess — there's a huge swell coming from one direction and big, choppy wind-driven waves from another. Every so often a big wave breaks over the boat, blanketing the cockpit enclosure and the deck with water.

"This is a proper North Atlantic gale," Chris says.

It's by far the worst weather we've seen since we left Antigua. Was it really only three weeks ago? There's nothing but open water behind us, 2,500 miles of it. That's a lot of room for the sea to build. Chris must be thinking the same thing.

"This gale could push us right past the Azores," he says grimly.

Chris checks our position on the GPS, then puts out a security call on the marine radio.

"Sailboat hove-to at 39, 27 north, 34, 55 west." He hangs up the mike.

"Come on," he says. "Let's go below."

I look at him, astonished.

"The boat can handle it," he says, "probably better than we can. Come on. We'd better get some rest."

I just can't. I follow him as far as the companionway, where I stand clutching the frame, looking out over the water. I can't see much—the wind is tearing the tops off the waves, filling the air with foam, and it's raining, hard.

I wonder what Dad would make of his daughter being out in a gale in the middle of the ocean. Or would make, if he knew where we were. I imagine him standing in front of the map in Mom's room, pushpin in hand, with no idea where to put it. I haven't been able to send him our position since we lost our SSB. The long piece of red yarn will just be dangling from a pushpin somewhere between Bermuda and the Azores.

This is out of my hands. There's nothing I can do. Bless this woman, I think. Bless this man. Keep them safe on the water.

I go below, strip off my wet foul-weather gear, hang it on the hook beside the open companionway. It drips on the floor, but there's nothing I can do about that, either. And it doesn't matter. The whole boat is soaked with salt water. When a wave breaks over the cockpit, a fine spray comes in through the companionway—there's a puddle at the foot of the ladder. Water drips from the ceiling in the salon, in the galley. Where is it coming from? We don't know. We thought the boat was waterproof. It isn't.

It's dim down below. Waves fill the portholes with water, then they empty, fill, empty, blocking out what light there is. And it's much quieter. The thick steel hull muffles the sound of the wind.

I check to make sure the abandon-ship kit is where it should be, within reach of the foot of the ladder. The life raft on deck is packed with the essentials—water and dried food, a blanket, a first aid kit, a fish hook and some line, a plastic cup for bailing, a mirror for signalling planes. But I've gathered together a few other things we might want if we find ourselves bobbing in a rubber raft in the middle of the ocean—a compass, a flashlight and extra batteries, a roll of toilet paper (clearly life rafts are designed by men), a bag of ginger candies for seasickness. A second cup for bailing.

Chris is stretched out on the starboard settee, a blanket pulled up to his chin. Neither of us has had a good wash in days, so his dark hair, much greyer now than when we set out, goes every which way, and his chin is covered with stubble. Do I see bits of grey in it, too?

Quietly as I can, I lie down on the bench across from him.

"What are you doing over there?"

"I didn't want to wake you."

"You think I'm sleeping? Come on over here." He shifts over, making room for me, lifts the blanket.

I snuggle in beside him. He tucks the blanket tightly around me so I won't fall out when the boat rolls. We're both exhausted, but neither of us can sleep.

"What are you thinking about?" he asks me.

"I didn't see it coming," I say drowsily.

"You're not talking about the gale, are you."

"No. I guess I'm not." I lie there in silence. He waits.

"I never told you the whole story. I've never told anyone. I didn't think it was mine to tell."

"So tell me now."

"It doesn't have a happy ending."

"I already know the ending. You and Emily in a condo in an old schoolhouse in Waterloo. I want to hear the whole story. Don't leave anything out."

I watch the brass lamp above the table swinging wildly. I hope the hook in the ceiling doesn't work free. What a mess that would make, oil all over the floor and worse, on our new leather cushions. Not that the boat isn't already a mess. We thought we were stowed for sea. We weren't. The door to the wet locker has flung open and the life jackets have spilled out. Books have tumbled off the shelves. A flashlight rolls back and forth, back and forth, across the cabin floor.

"We laughed when the medical social worker told us that fifty percent of marriages end within a year when one of the partners has an organ transplant. Not us, we said. Not us."

I hesitate. Chris pulls me a little closer, waits for me to go on.

"Brad had just had his six-month check-up. It was all good. But it wasn't. He was sullen, withdrawn. I could understand that. He'd been through so much. We were sitting in the backyard, looking at the garden I'd just planted—he was still too weak to do much yard work. The dogs were asleep in the grass at our feet, Chester now full grown.

"'I've given this a lot of thought,' he said suddenly. 'A new kidney doesn't last forever. They say I have maybe ten good years before it starts to deteriorate. I don't want to spend those years with you.'

"I was stunned. I felt like I'd been kicked in the stomach.

"'It's the drugs,' I said. 'The social worker said you shouldn't make any big decisions for at least a year. Let's wait and see how you feel then.'

"I wanted to take him back to London, ask them to treat him with anti-rejection drugs again, see if that would help."

A wave breaks over the boat with a mighty crash, and for a moment, the boat is still. We can hear the sound of water pouring out of the scuppers. Surely the seas are building.

"Just a minute," Chris says, disentangling himself from the blanket. He goes to the companionway, climbs up into the cockpit. A minute later he's back, damp but satisfied that everything is okay.

"Nothing broken," he says. "Nothing lost, that I can see. The preventers we rigged seem to be holding."

He climbs back in beside me.

"Now, where were we?"

"That last awful year. I should have left right away. It was like I wasn't there. He would get up in the morning and go to work without saying goodbye, work late, then eat his supper in front of his new big-screen TV, come to bed late. I didn't say anything, tried to give him time and space. He'd been through so much."

I look up at Chris. Does he really want to hear this? Do I really want to tell him?

"It's okay," he says.

"Slowly the sullenness turned into anger. Of course he's angry, I thought. None of this is fair. How would I feel if I had been so sick for so long, had come so close to dying? But the anger was a lot harder to live with than the cold withdrawal.

"I tried to stay out of his way. If he was having a bad day, I'd sit quietly in the living room, reading my book, or at least pretending to, while he watched TV. We no longer walked the dogs together. He would take Chester to the trail by the river on his way home from work and I would just walk Emily around the neighbourhood.

"One evening, he came home later than usual. Chester was limping a little.

"'What happened?'" I asked him.

"'He wouldn't come when I called him.'

"I didn't ask what happened next. I didn't want to know. I was afraid of him by then, to be honest.

"He began leaving Chester at home more often. When you were sick, I wanted to say to him, he was your constant companion, slept on the rug beside the bed when you rested, too sick to do anything else. He got you out for walks, which helped you stay strong. He mopes when you're not around, won't eat, hardly gets out of his bed. He needs more than a pat on the head from you each night. He can't survive on crumbs. He needs you to talk to him, go on long walks with him, be his best friend again."

"You're not talking about Chester, are you?" Chris says.

"Maybe not."

"I decided to start walking Chester myself, just around the neighbourhood, but the first time I did, two blocks away a Doberman threw itself against the wooden fence around the yard it was in, started jumping straight up in the air. I didn't know whether he was trying to escape and come after us or just jumping up to get a better look at us, but he was barking and snarling viciously, and I was terrified. I hurried back home, shaken and sick at heart about the state of my life.

"But still I waited, kept hoping he would come around."

Chris reaches over and stokes my hair.

"What finally made you decide to leave?"

"I didn't decide. He did. On the anniversary of his surgery, almost to the day.

"I had been away for the day, really just trying to stay out of his way. I came back to find him watching golf on TV. Chester was sprawled on the floor at his feet, but I couldn't find Emily.

"'Where is she?' I asked.

"'I don't know,' he said irritably.

"I heard a whimper from the front hall, found her curled up in a corner. She yelped with pain when I picked her up.

"'What happened?' I asked him.

"'I don't know.' He got up from the sofa. 'She and Chester were playing before.'

"It was after hours so we took her to an emergency vet, who sedated her and x-rayed her. Nothing was broken, and there was no internal bleeding. The vet told us to give her painkillers and keep her quiet for a couple of weeks. We weren't to let her climb stairs or jump up on anything.

"About a week later, as we were getting ready to go to his sister's place for Thanksgiving dinner, I said, 'Should we leave Emily at home? There are a lot of stairs at your sister's place, and we won't be able to watch her every minute. And what if her dog tries to play with her and she gets hurt again?'

"'That's it,' he snapped. 'It's over. I want you out right after Christmas.'

"There was never any doubt that I would have to be the one to go. Brad needed a driveway for his truck and Chester needed a big backyard. I didn't want to stay in the house alone anyway. It would be too sad."

Suddenly there is a loud crash in the galley. We both leap up, but Chris gets there first. The door to the baking cupboard has broken free and everything has spilled onto the floor of the galley—flour, oatmeal, raisins, brown sugar, worst of all. It's a crunchy, sticky mess.

"Leave it," Chris says. "We'll get it later."

We snuggle back in.

"I don't really understand what happened," I tell Chris.

"The door to the baking cupboard opened," he says with a straight face.

I give him a swat. "Not that.

"Maybe he was fighting to get back some control over his life, some dignity. I would always remind him of how vulnerable he had been, how dependent on me. I had to go. But I think he felt bad about ending things, after all we'd been through together, felt he had to find fault with me to justify his decision. He certainly did a good job of it.

"'You're too fearful,' he'd tell me. 'Too needy. Too high mainte-nance. Too controlling.' And on and on."

*You're out of shape. You should lose some weight. You're going to wear that?*

I pause, try to quiet the voice in my head.

"By the time I left, I felt completely worthless. I was afraid to look in the mirror in case there was nothing there."

Chris pulls me close to him.

"I see you," he whispers. "And I love you."

IT SEEMS QUIETER now, or maybe we've just grown used to the howling wind, the slap of water against the hull. The boat still rolls and rights, rolls and rights. Chris holds me tightly and we both drift off to sleep.

What light there was in the cabin has faded by the time I wake up. I slide out from under the blanket and, clutching the handles on the ceiling with both hands, monkey my way over to the nav station and sit down at the desk. I turn up the volume on the VHF radio, listen to make sure the hailing channel is clear, pick up the microphone.

"*Sécurité, sécurité, sécurité.* This is the sailing vessel *MonArk*. We are hove to at— " I read out the latitude and longitude on the GPS in front of me, then listen. No response, not even a bit of static.

Suddenly a big gust of wind heels us over. Surely it's at least fifty knots? Maybe more? The boat rights itself, and I can hear water streaming out through the scuppers. We're okay. For now. But the gale isn't letting up. And it's getting dark. And we're alone out here.

But I've never felt less alone.

*June 15*

~~~~~~

*Day 25*

"We've got to get moving."

"Huh?" I had been sound asleep.

"The wind has dropped," Chris says. He's already climbing the companionway ladder. "We've got to put out more sail."

I follow Chris above deck and see that there's no longer enough wind in the tiny bit of sail we have up to keep us stable. We're taking the waves on the bow, on the beam, on the bow again as we bounce around. Chris starts the engine, then moves the main over to the starboard side.

"We need to bring the genoa across," he says, loosing the sheet on the port side.

I grab the handle, crank in the sheet on the starboard side. He eases more sail out until we are balanced. Then, as we pick up speed, he adjusts our heading until he finds the most comfortable path through the waves. Fortunately, it turns out to be more or less in the direction of Flores. Unfortunately, we have drifted twenty-two miles farther away from the island.

Chris takes the first watch. I'm still a little nervous about the weather, don't quite trust that it's all over. Eighteen hours, I think as I finally drift off to sleep. The gale lasted eighteen hours.

I sleep soundly until 3:00 am, then relieve Chris and let him sleep. As morning breaks, the clouds that slowly emerge from the darkness are hazy at sea level but distinctly rounded higher up, dark blue above, lighter blue and white and almost yellow down below. I've never seen anything like it.

But the weather seems to clear a little as the day wears on. There are even a few brief sunny periods. We don't even try to clean up down below—we just sprawl in the cockpit, take turns napping on the bench. And I don't bother making any food—neither of us feels at all like eating. We just nibble on crackers, drink as much water as we can. We'll make landfall in the morning, we can clean up then, eat some real food. But not before we fall into bed together and sleep and sleep and sleep.

As dusk falls, I make us some tea, then send Chris below to try to get some sleep before his night watch. The clouds still look strange. I'm almost relieved when the light fails and I can't see them any more. The wind seems to be dropping. Just seventy-nine miles to go. Our last night at sea. We should be able to see Flores when dawn breaks.

I unzip the canvas windscreen, step up on the cockpit benches, lean on the dodger. It's cold, but I want to feel the wind in my hair, watch the bow cutting through the waves, sending water foaming along the sides of the boat.

"Look at me!" I shout. The wind snatches my words away. "I've been through a proper North Atlantic gale."

*June 16*

~~~~~~

*Day 26*

Chris has had a quiet watch, and I'm hoping for the same. Around 2:00 am the wind suddenly dies, and I think, good, we're out of it now, I'll bet when morning comes, the dark clouds will have disappeared. But an hour later, the wind suddenly starts to build.

I call Chris to help me reduce sail. We crank in the genoa almost all the way, tie a third reef in the main, just in time. A wall of wind hits us, like nothing either of us has ever felt before, on land or at sea. It must be at least sixty knots, well beyond gale force, verging on hurricane force winds.

"We need to heave to now," Chris says.

I don't like the edge in his voice.

I brace myself, and as we crest the next wave, Chris turns us into the wind. We need the bow to come across the wind in order to backwind the foresails and stall our forward motion, but it doesn't happen. As we come up on the wind, the boat picks up speed and heels over sharply, but the tiny slip of genoa we have out is too much. We can't get across. As the wave passes under us, the boat rolls on its side, the mast at a forty-five-degree angle to the water. A winch handle slides out of the cockpit, bounces on the cap rail and disappears into the foaming seas. The mainsail is flogging uncontrollably, the boom banging back and forth. The foresails are blocking its wind. Can the rig take this pounding? The boat is actually shuddering, something I've never felt before. I glance down the companionway at the abandon-ship kit.

When the wave has passed under us, Chris eases the wheel and we fall off the wind. The boat rights itself somewhat, and the main fills with wind. We're back where we started.

"We need to take in all of the genoa," Chris says, but he can't leave the helm.

It's not safe for me to go forward, so I have to crank it from the cockpit, inch by inch.

"Okay, now hold on," Chris says, needlessly. I'm holding on as hard as I can. "We're going to try again."

As we reach the top of the next wave, we heel over more than I would have thought possible, then suddenly we're across the wind. The mainsail tacks itself and fills with wind and the storm-sail backwinds, stalling the boat. Chris turns the rudder hard so it's working against the backwinded stormsail, then makes tiny adjustments to the wheel until we're taking the building seas at the best possible angle.

This time, Chris doesn't suggest that we go below. Wordlessly, we watch the rail on the leeward side flirting with the churning seas. My heart sinks. How high will the seas build in these winds? What will we do? I don't ask. If it doesn't capsize us, this wind could blow us past Flores, I think grimly, or worse, right onto its rocky cliffs. We can't reduce sail any further. Oh—we can. We watch as the wind tears our stormsail to shreds.

I've had enough of this. Maybe I'm not as brave as I thought.

*You're not.*

"Leave me alone," I mutter.

Then the wind dies as suddenly as it came up.

We can't believe our luck. Chris switches on the engine and starts motoring cautiously in the direction of Flores through very confused seas. I sit numbly beside him on the cockpit bench, staring through the windscreen. It's just starting to get light. The strange-coloured clouds are gone, replaced by low, ugly clouds. We can't see more than a mile ahead of us, if that.

We pick up Flores on the radar long before we can see it. On a clear day, the guidebook says, you can see Flores from forty miles away. We are just four miles from the island and we can't see anything but a dark bank of clouds where Flores should be.

Then I spot a funnel of white rising from the sea up into the dark clouds. Now what? A waterspout? Chris unzips the windscreen to get a better look, then he grins.

"Take a look."

What we're seeing is a waterfall plunging down the face of a cliff. Land! We're seeing land for the first time in almost a month. We have crossed 2,300 miles of ocean and ended up exactly where we wanted to be. Sure, we have a chart plotter, but the charts for the ocean aren't very detailed. And we have a GPS to confirm our position, and paper charts to mark where we are. But our arrival here is still a wonder to me. To both of us, I think.

IT TAKES US several hours to sail the length of Flores to the town of Lajes, the nearest shelter (the only real shelter) for sailboats. The island rises sharply from the sea, and much of the shoreline is studded with huge chunks of rock that have fallen from the cliffs, jagged teeth sticking out of the water. Where they're not sheer rock, the cliffs are covered in lush green foliage. Every inch of the land above, right to the edges of the cliffs, is divided into neat fields, lined with hedges and low stone walls. From the sea, it looks like a crazy quilt, the patches all different shades of green. We pass a tiny village, a handful of stone houses clinging to the top of a cliff. All the buildings have bright red roofs.

Lajes used to be a small, unprotected whaling port, but then a modern jetty was built for cargo boats and the ferries that run between islands, creating a small, deep-water anchorage behind it. Chris is concerned that in these confused seas, we may have trouble making the tight turn into the harbour, and we do have an anxious moment when we have to take the seas on the beam, but the boat just rolls, then rights itself once we're inside the stone jetty. To our dismay, the tiny anchorage is full—we aren't the only boat seeking shelter here.

"What do you think?" he says. "Between the American boat and the boat from the U.K.?"

"Looks pretty tight."

"Yeah, but we don't have much choice. There's room for us to fall back behind them a bit. We'll be pretty close to the quay, but that will make for a shorter dinghy ride to shore."

Chris glances down at the depth reading. "Holy cow," he says. "Fifty feet. We're going to have to let out all of our chain." He gives me the wheel, goes forward to drop anchor. "Just keep us on the wind."

I try, but the wind keeps shifting around. I'm glad when we fall back a little, out of range of the boats beside us. I keep a careful eye on the quay behind us. We're not used to having solid objects around us.

At the sound of our chain running out, people appear on the decks of the boats already at anchor.

"You sailed through this?" one man shouts, incredulous.

We did. And we look like we did.

I have photos of us taken just before we made landfall. We are both wearing our yellow rain gear, looking none the cleaner for the long journey. Chris has about a week's worth of whiskers on his face and his hair is plastered to his head. He looks exhausted, but he's smiling, and there's a gleam of satisfaction in his eyes.

It's impossible to gauge the state of my hair. It's all tucked up under my lucky Herbert Fisheries cap, and I have the hood of my raincoat up. I had been looking out the open side panel, watching the island emerge from the gloom, but I've turned to look at Chris. My face is wet with rain or salt spray, it's hard to say which, and my cheeks are pink with the cold, but I'm smiling—looking a bit smug, actually. We did it! We did it.

# LANDFALL

BY THE TIME THE ANCHOR IS SET, THE OFFICIALS ARE WAITING ON the quay. Our first impulse is to fall into bed and sleep for a day, but the Portuguese are very strict about marine protocol—the captain must go ashore and clear in. We launch the dinghy, which has been lashed upside down on the foredeck since we left Antigua. Then Chris grabs our papers, runs his fingers through his hair, climbs down the ladder, and he's off.

I'm not happy that we're hanging with our stern towards shore. I sit in the cockpit, keeping a careful eye on the stone quay behind us. If we drag, we'll be on it in no time. But so far, the anchor seems to be holding.

It feels so strange to be still—well, relatively still, anyway. And to have something to look at other than water and sky. The new jetty is ugly—a long finger of concrete sticking out into the ocean, big pieces of formed concrete tumbled along the outside edge to break the waves. But it protects us from the huge ocean swell and confused seas. The harbour is wide open to the east, though, which is where the wind is coming from. For the most part, we're staying nose to the wind, taking the waves on the bow, but from time to time the boat dances around as a gust of wind plunges down the high cliffs that line the coast.

It also feels strange to be alone after a month at sea with this man. I feel like my arm or a leg or certainly a piece of my heart has just left in a dinghy. I scan the quay, hope he's made it safely—yes, there he is, talking to a man wearing a navy jacket and a peaked cap.

I check the anchor again, then settle back with the binoculars and study the cliffs that line the shore. Narrow, jagged plumes of water plunge over the top of them. I wonder if they are always there or just appear when there's been a heavy rain. They're not waterfalls, really, more like downspouts. The seabirds that nest on the cliffs here aren't happy about them. They circle the harbour, calling angrily. Or maybe that's how they always sound.

On the jagged rocks at the base of the cliffs, I notice a rusty steel sailboat being slowly pounded to pieces. Did they drag anchor? I wonder. Or maybe their engine failed as they were trying to claw their way out of the harbour in a gale like the one we just came through. Imagine making it all the way across the ocean only to be shipwrecked this close to shore. I hope they got off safely.

Before long Chris is back.

"We're in," he says. He checks the pattern the boat is making on the chart plotter as we swing from side to side. A nice black semicircle, a smile. The anchor is well and truly set.

"Come on. Let's go for a quick walk before we crash."

It takes me a few minutes to find my running shoes. I put on a cleaner shirt, one I haven't slept in, run a hand through my hair—I know I'm a mess, but I can't wait to get ashore.

"Let's go."

Chris knows the way now. He heads for the old slipway, tucked behind the quay. There are steps on one side, which allow people to climb ashore regardless of the tide. Well, not exactly regardless. You have to take a lot more care at low tide. The bottom steps, which are underwater most of the time, are covered with green slime. Chris noses the dinghy up to them and holds it against them with the engine while I step ashore with the line. I'm glad I took the time to put on my running shoes. My first step on European "soil" is a slippery one. I manage to keep my feet as I hold the dinghy close enough for Chris to disembark.

"Ewww," he says, wiping slime from his hand.

He ties the line to a rusty iron ring—how old, I wonder—and we carefully make our way up the steps to the foot of the old sea wall. I can't believe this used to be the village's only protection from the wild North Atlantic. I'm sure that in the gales of winter, waves break over this twenty-foot-high wall, even with the new jetty. I don't think those drainage holes along the top are just for rainwater.

We begin the long climb to the village, the ground swaying beneath our feet. Up and up we go, stopping to rest from time to time. We've been at sea for almost a month. The farthest we've walked is forty-three feet, and that not very often. I feel lightheaded and a little ill. I've heard that it takes as long to get your land legs as it does to get your sea legs, so I'm in for at least three days of this. But I don't care. I'm happy to be on solid ground, to be walking on cobblestone for the first time in my life. I am in Europe, or at least a tiny fragment of Europe out in the Atlantic Ocean.

We stop at the library to send a quick email home—we made it!—and find a message from Chris Parker in our inbox.

"It appears the low does not dip as far south as I thought... so you get clobbered by the front overnight tonight. Expect 40-knot winds and squalls late this evening. Hang on... it only lasts 6–12 hours, then things moderate."

"Would have been good to know," Chris says with a grin.

There's a message from Brenda, too—I download it to read later. We follow the road up to the church, crossing a stone bridge over a stream that has cut a channel deep into the rock through the middle of town. We stop in front of the church to admire it—and catch our breath—then continue our climb, up and out of the village.

We're both getting tired, but we walk a little way out into the countryside. There are flowers everywhere, hydrangeas growing in thick hedges along the road, roses climbing rusted farm gates. It seems a bit early to me, but the Queen Anne's lace along the road is just starting to bloom, and there are tiger lilies growing in the ditch. It's just like the farm. And yet so not like it.

The land here is divided into small fields separated by low stone walls. Most of them are pasture, with cows and sheep grazing on them. We meet a man leading a bull, a huge red animal that submits meekly to the rope around his neck. He could easily break free but shows no inclination to, not surprising considering what the man is leading him to—or from. There are milking machines out in the fields, rusty old mechanical devices. Clearly they milk the cows out in the pastures, which is perhaps why the cows look at us so expectantly as we pass.

But we can't walk any farther—our legs are starting to feel wobbly. We turn back to the village, stop at a little store beside the road—the front room of a house, actually.

"*Pão?*" the woman behind the counter asks.

We look at each other. What could she mean? She goes through the door to the house, comes back with a fresh loaf of bread.

"Yes, please," I say.

No that's not right. What's the Portuguese word for yes? It doesn't matter. She understands. We pick up a bag of ripe plums and some soft cheese to go with the bread, then head back down to the harbour with our purchases.

At the top of the sea wall, we stop to admire our boat bobbing at anchor in the harbour below. It feels good to be viewing it from a distance.

"Look at that," Chris says. There is a French boat sailing straight into the crowded anchorage, a woman at the helm, a man standing at the bow. The woman shouts something and lets the jib sheet go, spilling the wind from the foresail. The man drops the anchor, and when it grabs, the boat spins around into the wind. They're down.

"Show-offs," Chris says, enviously.

Exhausted now, we head back to the boat for some supper—fresh bread!—and a good night's sleep. Tomorrow we'll attempt to bring some semblance of order to the boat.

THE NEXT MORNING, we make many trips to the public sink at the base of the sea wall where fishermen clean their catch. We lug jugs of fresh water back to the boat, wash all the hatches and portholes and rinse the salt out of our clothes, hang them in the rigging to dry. Then we pack a couple of bottles of water in a backpack and what remains of the bread and cheese and dinghy to shore.

There is a woman at the sink, up to her elbows in cold water, rinsing the salt out of diapers and tiny shirts and pairs of pants, little dresses, a grey teddy bear, an only-slightly-less-grey bunny, blankets, sheets, towels. Her hands are red and raw, her brown curly hair falls in her eyes. So intent is she on her task that we pass her by without a greeting, not sure what language to use in any case. She doesn't look Portuguese.

With a little more confidence in our legs than we had the day before, we climb the path to the village, through the square, then up, up out of the village and along the coastal road, which is lined with a low stone wall tangled with pink roses.

The church in the next village is covered in blue and white tiles, a sharp contrast to the rough stone and plaster on the houses surrounding it. To our surprise, it's unlocked. We push the heavy wooden door open, and inside is an altar draped with lace and heavy with flowers—lilies, for the most part, mixed with ferns. The elaborate plaster work is thick with gold.

School has let out by the time we leave the church and children have gathered in the shade of the big tree in the village square.

"Good afternoon," one of the little boys says formally. Then he giggles, no doubt feeling as self-conscious as we do when we try to speak Portuguese.

"*Boa tarde*," I say, trying to roll the "r" and swallow the "d" the way I heard the woman in the store do it. The children dissolve into fits of laughter.

Farther along the coastal road we come to a ceramic sign (all the signs are ceramic here, white tiles with blue writing and pictures of flowers). We can't read it, of course, but we see the word "natur" so we decide to follow the overgrown trail plunging down the side of a ravine.

We pick our way down an ancient cobblestone cart path that quickly degenerates into a series of moss-covered steps descending to a fast-moving stream. Along the stream are the ruins of several old buildings. Houses? Mills maybe? Each building is about the size of a garden shed and has a millstone worn smooth by years of use. Clearly the settlement was deserted long ago—but what was it doing here in the first place? I can't imagine a less accessible spot. Or a more beautiful one.

We sit on the doorstep of one of the buildings, watch a grey wagtail work his way along the boulders beside the river, laugh at the way he pumps his tail, admire his yellow chest—he's in full breeding plumage. The water gurgles by our feet. Only dappled sunlight makes its way to the bottom of the ravine. It's perfectly quiet except for the birds.

Suddenly I'm ten years old, riding my bike as fast as I can along the trail beside the river. I'm not supposed to be here when I'm on my own—there are tramps, my mother says, whatever they are. And what if I fall off my bike and hurt myself? She doesn't know what a great rider I am, how fast I can go on my palomino.

*Really?*

Yes.

I'm heading for the deep ravine where the creek feeds into the river, another place I'm not supposed to go—there could be boys playing there, wild dogs even. But I don't care. It's Easter Sunday, all the eggs have been found (hidden in the living room, not outside, even though it's a warm, sunny day). Mom and Dad are sitting at the kitchen table, smoking, drinking coffee. My mother's coffee has gone cold, but she says she likes it that way. The other kids are watching TV, except for my new baby brother, Dave, who is securely fastened in a towel pinned to the back of the couch because he keeps trying to crawl outside. But I don't feel too sorry for him—he's happy enough there, for now, bouncing, gurgling, waving his hands.

I've slipped away and I'm on an adventure. I have a hard-boiled egg and hot-cross bun tucked in one pocket, the last of my chocolate bunny—the ears—tucked in the other. I have everything I need.

That ten-year-old girl lost her way somehow, I think to myself, as I watch a tiny chaffinch perched on a low bush singing his heart out. But she's finding her way back.

AS WE RETRACE our steps along the coastal road, we stop from time to time to look out over the now perfectly benign-looking ocean. Sunlight sparkles on the deep blue water. There's almost no wind. Off in the distance we see a tiny sailboat—heading to the harbour here? It's making very slow progress.

It's late when we get back to Lajes so we decide to stop at Paula's, the only café in town, for supper. As we cut through the garden beside the church, we walk by the woman we saw down at the sea wall. She's sitting on a bench, a book open in her hands, a Portuguese dictionary. Definitely not Portuguese, then. Again she is too absorbed in her task for us to disturb her. She doesn't even look up as we pass.

Paula serves us plates of salted codfish and potatoes stewed in some kind of wonderful tomato sauce, which we wash down with local beer. Exhausted by our day's hike, we head back to the boat. As we walk down to the harbour, we notice that the French boat has been lifted onto the quay. It's missing its rudder. A man and woman — ah, the woman with the brown curly hair — are unloading all their belongings into a container. They don't look very happy. Two children are playing half-heartedly around the boat. The little boy is fending off an imaginary enemy with a wooden sword that is too big for him — he can hardly lift it. Indifferent to the fact that they are under attack, his sister struts around in a long pink skirt and feathered hat. The man calls down to them and they put their toys in the container.

As we dinghy back to the boat, Chris spots a boat sailing somewhat erratically back and forth just outside the harbour.

"I wonder if he's in trouble," he says.

When we get to our boat, Chris puts out a call on the VHF and asks if everything is all right.

"I could use some help," a tired voice responds.

Chris climbs back in the dinghy and zips out of the harbour. I watch him pull alongside the boat, then tie the dinghy to it and climb aboard. I can't really make out what they're doing — the boat continues to sail back and forth across the mouth of the harbour, the dinghy in tow. Then I see Chris climb back in the dinghy and zoom towards me. He stops long enough to give me a quick update.

"Nice guy, named Niles. He was hammered by the same gale we were. His batteries are dead, his engine won't turn over, and his boom is broken. He's been hand steering for days now and he's totally exhausted. Without the main, we can't get the boat to point

into the wind enough to make the turn into the harbour. I'm going
to shore to get some help."

He returns in about fifteen minutes, climbs on board.

"I talked a fishing boat into going out to get him."

"How did you do that?" I tease him.

"With a lot of hand gestures."

THE NEXT DAY, while Chris tries to repair our shredded stormsail,
I settle down in the cockpit to read Brenda's letter. It's a long one.

Dear Linda

I hope by the time you read this you've had an uneventful
last few days at sea and have made landfall in the Azores. I
made a pretty spectacular landfall myself this week... It's a
long story, so go make yourself a cup of tea.

Anna and I went shopping for riding clothes Friday night,
after school. We bought her a pair of riding breeches and tall
riding boots—like the rubber boots you bought me, but
without the red strip around the top. All second hand—very
sensible for a growing child. The breeches have leather patches
inside the knee to enhance hanging-on ability and also to
prevent saddle burn. She looked cute as a bug in them but of
course that was not any part of the decision to get her proper
riding attire, no sir.

But here's the part I think you will understand, Linda, like
no one else would.

I wanted a pair of breeches too, because I ride in old black
pants that are comfortable enough, but they fall down when
I'm standing up so I need to hike them up all the time, and
the legs ride up, so I need to lean over and pull the pantlegs
down when I'm riding. All around unsuitable riding attire.
And black is too hot in warm weather. Anyway, those were the
excuses. I wanted sleek, beige leather-patched breeches, so I
got a lovely pair, brand new because I am not a growing child.
They even make my butt look good!

Then, in a moment of excitement and indulgence, I bought a pair of leather half-chaps—no, not the things of cowboy fantasies...they fit over your calf from ankle to knee, zip up outside with a neat snap closure at top and bottom. They also have a little strap that goes under your boot, like ski-pants did in the old days. So they provide a sleek leather sleeve from heel to knee. Their purpose is to reduce any places for rubbing between your boots and pants, keep the pants from riding up, and well, they look so darned smart! I picked chocolate brown suede to go with my camel-coloured breeches and already brown boots. I was so proud and embarrassed at the same time.

Then of course I had doubts all night about wearing them to the barn the next day. It seemed so silly for a beginner to buy expensive breeches and chaps ($150!). Who did I think I was? But by morning I had tried them on so many times that I was ready to nonchalantly show up in my new stuff. Anna, however, gleefully showed off her new tall boots and breeches, saying they make her look at least seven years old, and pointed out Mommy's new attire. The instructor took me aside and very kindly murmured that I had the chaps on backwards.

It sure did make a difference riding. I could hold on better and feel the movement of the horse better. Which didn't help me one bit when my horse tripped over his own big feet going over a jump in a corner and fell to his knees.

He recovered himself quickly and I would have been fine, Linda, except that in my nervousness approaching the corner, I hadn't put my hands far enough forward on his mane so when he went down, I went right over his head, did a somersault, and landed hard, really hard, on my hip and back. I rolled and got up, worried that he would bolt and trample me, but he was standing right over me, calmly, looking very puzzled.

I was okay, but quite shaken. Anna, on the other hand, was in complete hysterics, having watched me fall. I walked over and had a few quiet words with her, then walked her around on her pony for a bit to work out the kinks in my back and settle her down. We agreed that I was now officially a rider, and I got back on my horse and finished the lesson, even though all I wanted to do was go home and cry.

I picked up groceries on the way home, cooked a nice supper, spent a quiet evening with Anna then put her to bed. Finally I took some painkillers and crawled into bed and had a big cry. Here's where I got stuck, Linda.

I felt so embarrassed. Who did I think I was in my fancy riding clothes? I'm really just a scared chicken. What if I lose my nerve and can't ride next week? What if I can't get over being scared of that corner?

But here's the worst one: What if Anna fell and got hurt? It would be my fault for keeping her in riding lessons. She likes riding, but I'm not so sure she loves it like I do. She seems to enjoy the other girls more than the horses. What if I'm placing her in the way of danger just because I love to ride? What kind of a mother am I? I would never forgive myself if she got seriously hurt.

So it has been a weird few days. I feel like a foolish middle-aged woman. Maybe this is what a mid-life crisis looks like: a grown woman doing a child's sport, with a huge blue bruise on my leg where it hit the saddle going over, and Advil and heating pads on my back for three days. How foolish is that??

My back will get better—it's getting better already—and the bruise is spectacular but fine. I am slightly less afraid of going riding next Saturday (even looking forward to it, to be honest). But I feel shaken inside, because what if I cannot tell the difference between excitement and adventure, and stupidity? What if this is just stupid? Or worse, what if it is not stupid, but I let fearfulness stop me from having an adventure? And the very worst of all: how do I know the difference?

How I wish you were here and we could talk this through. I'm sure you know something about this... But of course you are probably busy exploring the Azores. I can't wait to hear what it's like there.

Love you.
Beek

I WISH WE could talk, too. Always go for the adventure, I want to tell her. But even a short call on the satphone costs about fifty dollars. I close my computer, go below to put it away and to let Chris know I'm going to shore to pick up some fresh bread for our lunch. He doesn't look up. He's muttering at the sewing machine, the thread has broken again. I'm glad to have an errand.

On the way back to the harbour, I pass the French woman, who is again studying her dictionary, this time on a stone bench at the top of the sea wall. She's alone—I can see her children playing on the quay below us. Her husband pokes his head out of the container from time to time to check on them.

I work up the courage to approach her.

"I think I spoke to you out in the ocean," I say shyly.

She looks up. Her eyes are dark brown, almost black.

"Yes, you are from *MonArk*. I give you bad informations. The storm was very big."

"Sometimes it's better not to know. But we did okay. Better than that boat," I say, pointing to the one on the rocks below us.

Her English is better than my French, but between the two languages we manage, switching back and forth as we struggle to find the right words.

"We did not so good," she says. "Our—" She gestures with her hand.

"Rudder?" I offer.

"Yes. Is broken, and our engine too. And everything wet, so much salt!"

I point to her dictionary. "You are learning Portuguese?"

"Yes, to talk to the *capitão* and the men who must work on my boat. It is easy for me, more easy than English."

I look down at the quay. There is a mechanic's truck beside her boat, and a group of men are hoisting a new rudder into place. She must be doing okay.

"I do not think it will be ready soon," she says. "My husband must go home to start his job, and the children must go to school. I will stay here, sail the boat back."

"By yourself?" I ask her. "You did a great job of sailing into the harbour. Not many people could do that. Have you sailed alone before?"

"No, but I am excited to do it. I may just keep going," she says with a grin. "I said we will sail for a year, and then I will be a good doctor's wife. We will buy a house in a small village. I will take care of the children."

Her brow furrows. She looks down at her boat. It could go either way, I think.

"And you? Do you keep sailing?"

"Yes," I say. "The boat is our home now. We quit our jobs, sold our house, our cars. We will spend the summer here, go to Portugal for the winter, then into the Mediterranean next spring. I would like to spend some time in France, sail to Italy. Then who knows. Maybe Greece? Turkey?"

"So you are both sailors? My husband doesn't like so much to sail."

"I wasn't a sailor when I met him, but I think I am now."

"And how did you met him?"

"It's a long story."

"I have time," she says, closing her book.

I set the bag of rolls on the bench beside me, put my feet up on the sea wall. The sun is warm on our faces the wind teases our hair. She watches my face, waits. I have missed having a woman to talk to. Maybe it's that, or maybe it's something about the way she holds my gaze, leans slightly toward me, as though she doesn't want to miss a word. I find myself opening up to her.

I tell her I was living alone in my condo with my little dog when I met him, tell her a bit about my marriage, about how shattered I was when it ended.

"You had broken your heart," she says.

"Yes."

Then I tell her how kind Chris was to me, how good that felt. I was completely unguarded with him. I had decided never to get involved with a man again, never again to let anyone close enough to hurt me.

"We were just friends," I tell her. "And anyway, I learned long ago never to trust a man as good-looking as he is." People often stop Chris on the street and ask him if he's Richard Gere. Which is just silly. He's much better looking than Richard Gere.

"Yes." She smiles. "He is too handsome. So when did your mind change?"

"The first time he took me sailing."

I look down at our boat and I can see Chris standing on the stern, looking towards shore. He's wondering where I am. Or at least where his lunch is.

"I must go," I say, standing, picking up my bag of rolls.

"*À bientôt*," she says. "I like this, to talk to you."

"Me too."

CHRIS HAS SPENT the morning trying to help Niles start his engine. He has lots to tell me. It turns out Niles is at the tail end of an around-the-world cruise. He bought his boat on an impulse, intending to sail from England to Australia, where he had a contract to work for a few months. He signed up for a two-week sailing course before setting out across the English Channel. Two weeks.

He went from harbour to harbour down the coast of Europe, but he didn't like the looks of the African coast so he just kept going. When he reached the Cape of Good Hope, he holed up for several weeks, spending most of his time in the pub, in theory waiting for the right weather to round the treacherous point. One night the bartender told him it was time to go, so he just left and sailed all the way to Australia. In one shot. On his own.

After he finished his work in Australia, he just kept on going—across the South Pacific, up the coast of South America, through the Panama Canal to the Caribbean, then across the Atlantic to the Azores.

"He's on his way back to England now," Chris says, "but it's funny—even after circumnavigating the globe, he considers himself a computer programmer, not a sailor. And he may be right. He said he was knocked down in the gale—just a minor knockdown. I asked him what that looked like, and he said, 'You know, when the whole sail doesn't go in the water, just part of it.'"

Our sail has never been anywhere near the water.

"What were you and the French woman talking about for so long?" Chris asks. "I thought I was going to have to make my own lunch."

I tell him about her long list of repairs.

"We're pretty lucky, aren't we?"

"Not lucky," he says. "We have a sturdy boat."

"And you're a real sailor."

"So are you now. You've sailed more miles than most people do in a lifetime."

He's right. I *am* a sailor now. I have sailed across the ocean.

"Hey," I say, "Come to shore with me. There's something I need to do."

He eyes the bag of rolls hungrily but doesn't question me. We dinghy to shore, where I take his hand and lead him out along a country road. I have a pair of scissors in my pocket, which I use to cut a huge armload of hydrangeas.

"No one will miss a few of these."

Back at the boat, I fill several jars with water, place big bouquets of purple blossoms on the table, in the galley, in the bedroom. The lilacs at the farm pale in comparison, just a distant memory now.

"There," I say. "That's perfect. Let me make you some lunch."

THAT NIGHT I can't fall asleep, thinking about the French woman. I try to picture her living in an old stone cottage beside a river. Her backyard is overgrown with French lilacs, which I've never seen, only imagined. Her next-door neighbour tells her she should prune them but she can't bring herself to do it. Her husband is off on a call—do country doctors still make house calls in France? Now that both her children are in school, how does she spend her days? Does she pour herself a cup of coffee, stare out the window? I think she goes swimming in the cold river, and goes for long bike rides when the sun shines and even when it doesn't.

I give up on sleep, get up quietly, make myself a cup of milky tea. Maybe that will help. My mother used to drink a glass of warm milk every night before she went to bed. I can't quite bring myself to drink warm milk, but my tea has been getting milkier and milkier over the years. I'm sure that day will come.

I take my cup of tea above deck, and a blanket, and my computer—I'll write to Brenda. I curl up on the foredeck with my back against the mast, tuck the blanket around me, listen to the strange calls of shearwaters jostling for position on the cliff face behind me, look up at the night sky.

I think Brad loved me once. Where does it go? Is it a gradual thing, I wonder, does it just fade away? Or is it a sudden thing, like my mother's stroke—one minute you're fine, the next everything changes.

I see a blinking light overhead; it's a tiny plane moving across the sky, heading out over the Atlantic. I think of Chris's father in his Tiger Moth, helmet and goggles in place, silk scarf tied firmly around his neck, heading out on his first solo flight across the English Channel. Was it cold up there, I wonder? Did his leather jacket keep him warm enough? Did he bring a sandwich and a thermos of tea? I pull the blanket more tightly around my shoulders.

I don't understand how a plane can fly. Sure, something like Frank's little biplane makes sense, like a kite, only bigger. But the fighter planes he flew during the war were much more substantial—I've seen pictures of them—and much less plausible to me. I don't know how he made it to the end of the war without crashing or getting shot out of the sky. But I'm glad he did.

He was almost ninety when I met him. Get a haircut, were the first words he said to Chris when he opened the door. Stand up straight, Dad, Chris said. Then he introduced me. I don't know how you keep finding these nice girls, his father muttered as he led us to the living room. I found this flattering and more than a little disconcerting.

Though he kept asking when Chris was going to get a real job, I think Frank was secretly pleased that his son was setting off to sail across the ocean. He did the same thing when he was a young man, earned his passage by shovelling cattle manure on a cargo ship bound for England. Then he joined the Royal Air Force.

He must see something of himself in Chris, his youngest, the son who looks most like him, and I can certainly see him in Chris. I think Chris will be a grumpy old man, frustrated by his shaky legs, by how small his life has become. I reach over and pat his hand. Would you like more tea? What did you say? Quit mumbling. I pour him some tea anyway, go back to my book. He gets up and puts another log on the fire. At least that's how I hope it goes.

It's too cold on the foredeck, so I move into the cockpit, settle myself on the bench with the blanket over my legs. I open my computer, turn off the alarm. No need to scan for boats here.

Dear Brenda,

Yes, my dear, we did make it to the Azores, as you'll know by now. I hope the brief note I sent to everyone when we made landfall put your mind at ease. I made light of the gales we came through—it was actually pretty intense. But here we are, bobbing peacefully at anchor in the sort of sheltered harbour at Lajes. We're open to the east here, so if another front comes through we'll have to get out of here in a hurry. But for now we're just fine.

I hope by now the bruises on your backside have started to fade. Your bruised pride will take a little longer, I suspect. I understand perfectly what you're going through. The only thing more foolish than a middle-aged woman taking up horseback riding is a fifty-year-old running away with a sailor. I think I win on that one.

After I read your letter, I kept thinking about a friend of mine who was paralyzed by anxiety at the thought of buying a new couch. People will know that you wanted a new couch, she explained, and that you chose that particular one.

It takes a lot of courage to reach for the things you want, Beek. It's so much easier to just keep using the second-hand couch that came with the place or work in your garden or sit in an armchair in your condo reading biographies of women who actually did something with their lives.

When you do extend your reach, it's absolutely thrilling. You feel so alive. But when there's a little setback, a very nasty little voice, the one that kept my friend from buying a new couch, says, "Who do you think you are? What made you think you could have *that*? Sit down. Be quiet. Be good."

I have struggled with that voice all the way across the ocean. At first I thought it was just Mom's voice ringing in my ears. Be careful! What are you doing out in a storm? Get inside. Go to the basement. Stay there. It's the only safe place.

Then it started to turn nasty. What are you doing out here? Look at you. You're pathetic. Afraid of everything. What did you think was going to happen?

But here's a funny thing. That voice started to quiet once I told Chris about that horrible last year with Brad. You remember what he was like. You couldn't stand it when he berated me, which he wasn't afraid to do in front of company. You and Chuck stopped coming round to the house. I don't blame you.

I still hear his voice, from time to time, and on bad days, I still wonder if he was right. What if I am too emotional, too fearful, too needy? Worthless. Unloveable.

But telling Chris the story was freeing, somehow. Maybe I had to put a whole ocean between Brad and me before I began to feel that it was my story, too—that I had the right to tell it. And now that I have, I hear his voice less and less. It feels finished, somehow. I feel like I've put it behind me. And it feels good.

So you tell that voice to shut up, Beek. The joy you get out of riding that magnificent horse, the way you feel so happy and alive in your new riding pants and chaps and boots — the people you imagine would think you are ridiculous (do they even exist, I wonder?) will never know how alive it makes you feel.

And don't worry about the fear part — I have felt afraid, Brenda, many times on this journey. I tend not to talk about it because I don't want you to worry about me. (Will I tell you about some of our most frightening moments sometime?)

But, holy cow, it's worth it, eh?

I can't tell you what it felt like when the island first emerged from the mist and I realized that we had made it, we had sailed across the ocean, just the two of us. As Dory would say, it's a big ocean!

It's so beautiful here, Beek. The village we're anchored below (the island rises steeply from the water) is a collection of stone houses with red tile roofs, dominated by a huge church. Every house has a garden — no, every house *is* a garden. Every square inch of earth is planted with something. There are tomatoes growing in the front yards, and lettuce and onions and beans and potatoes. And flowers everywhere: roses, canna lilies, hydrangeas — these are just a few of the flowers I recognize. There are many more that I don't. I'm sure you would know what they are.

We've done some exploring already, and we plan to stay here as long as the weather stays settled. Then we're going to sail from island to island here in the Azores, taking our time, moving when the winds are favourable, staying put when they're not. At the end of August we'll sail to the south of Portugal, where we'll spend the winter. It's a one-week crossing at most, which seems like nothing — and frankly, everything — right now. I've had enough of big seas for a while.

Then who knows what? We're making it up as we go along.

I do hope you can come visit us in Portugal. I miss your face so much.

Love,
Linda

I CLOSE MY computer, look up at the night sky. Another plane is passing overhead. We must be on some kind of flyway here.

Modern planes don't make any more sense to me than WWII fighter planes. I wonder each time I'm in one if flying is really just an illusion that can and will pass. Sometimes I feel the same way about sailing. Why does a twenty-ton steel boat float? Are we just fooling ourselves? And what about love, what about happily after?

The blinking lights get smaller and smaller as the plane heads out over the ocean. May the illusion last, I say to myself. At least until that little plane makes it to the other side.

# HARD AGROUND

CHRIS SPRINGS OUT OF BED TRAILING THE BLANKET BEHIND HIM. Holy cow, I think, he really has to go. Then I hear the engine start, a clear sign when you're at anchor that something is really wrong.

"We're on the beach," he shouts as he runs forward to pull the anchor.

I can barely hear him above the howling wind, but I can see the beach just off our port beam. Another few feet and we'll be on our side.

We're weathering our first levanter in a little estuary on the Atlantic coast of Spain called Sancti-Petri. Though the channel is narrow, holding is good, we've been assured. And our anchor set firmly and held fast as the winds built — twenty-five, thirty, thirty-five knots, gusts to forty sometimes. Around midnight we went to bed, sure that we were well down and certain that if there was a problem, the anchor alarm would alert us. It hadn't let us down. Yet.

Well, we now know that when gale-force winds are screaming through the rigging, you can't hear the anchor alarm from down below. We also know that when the tide changes in Sancti-Petri, the current runs so swiftly it can pop your anchor out of the sand. If this happens in a levanter, you're on the beach in no time.

Chris tries to drive us off, but with no luck — the keel is buried in the sand.

"Take the helm," he shouts. "I'm going to try to kedge us off."

He climbs into the dinghy, zooms to where the anchor is dangling from the bow, grabs it and drops it some distance ahead of us. He climbs back onto the boat, runs to the foredeck, tries to winch us towards it but the anchor just skips along the bottom. We're running out of options, when suddenly it digs in. The boat lurches and I feel the keel pop out of the sand.

"Get us out of here!" Chris shouts.

I'm already gunning for the middle of the channel.

It's just light enough to make out the markers that will guide us out of the estuary, through the shifting sandbars and jagged reefs to open water. So although it's still early, we decide to get underway rather than re-anchoring. I go below to make us some coffee.

"That was close," Chris says as I hand him his cup.

"Yeah," I agree. "So much for one last quiet night at anchor. You got the next red, over there?"

I point to a marker up ahead, just off to our left.

"Yep."

The sun is starting to rise, the clouds above the low coastal hills washed with pink. We're both quiet — tired, sure, but it's more than that. We're on our way home, which is both heartbreaking and embarrassing.

You can't just sail away, our friends and families told us. Oh, yeah? Just watch us. We really did think we could sail forever, living on my writing and the modest income from Chris's company. We would live cheaply, at anchor most of the time, only going into marinas occasionally to wash our clothes and fill our water tanks. We would catch fish, buy bread and fresh produce in little villages along the coast, splurge on the occasional bottle of wine. It would be perfect. And it was. Until it wasn't.

After a peaceful summer in the Azores, sailing from one island to another, from one sheltered anchorage to the next, we headed to the mainland, where we waited out the winter storms nestled in a marina on the south coast of Portugal. On a bad day it was cold enough to wear a light jacket, but no colder, and it was almost always sunny.

Spring comes early in the Algarve, and in February, we started poking our way along the southern coast of Portugal, then down the Atlantic coast of Spain to the Strait of Gibraltar. By May we'd reached the Balearics, a group of islands in the western Mediterranean, where we planned to spend the summer sailing from anchorage to anchorage, from island to island, before heading to Italy, Rome maybe, for the winter.

But things weren't working out the way we had planned. So far I had sold just one magazine article, and that only because my dad went to see the editor of *Grand*, a glossy new lifestyle magazine in Kitchener-Waterloo. I'm sure he told her all about his dream of sailing away, in great detail. "And that's exactly what my daughter has done," I can hear him saying.

She may have agreed to the article just to get him out of her office.

Chris wasn't doing any better. In fact, his company was quietly going broke. Sales had dried up since he left and the company was deep into its line of credit. It was hard to ignore the fact that we were running out of money.

There is a photograph of me walking on the beach in Formentera, the smallest and least developed of the Balearic Islands. Behind me, the deep blue waters of the Mediterranean fade to light blue, then white as waves break onto the impossibly clean sand. The next island, Ibiza, is just visible in the background.

It is a beautiful sunny day, cool and windy. I'm wearing a purple fleecy and my hair is tied back in a ponytail, the carefully trimmed layers and highlights long since grown out. A few wisps of hair have escaped and blow around my face, which is grim. We have finally admitted to ourselves that we have to go home.

"If we head back now, we should be able to make it home before the hurricane season begins," Chris had said uncertainly. I didn't much like the sounds of that "should."

"Or we can spend the summer here, live as cheaply as we can, run the line of credit to the max, then put the boat on the hard, go home, and dig ourselves out."

I liked the sounds of that a lot better.

By the time we made it to Menorca, the easternmost of the Balearic Islands, we had about $100 dollars cash left and just enough room on our credit cards to buy two plane tickets home. Reluctantly, we turned back, retracing our path down the Mediterranean coast of Spain and back through the Strait.

Sancti-Petri was our last stop before the boatyard in Lagos, a little village at the westernmost tip of Portugal, where we'll pull the boat out of the water and put it in storage while we fly home.

But not before we spend one last night at sea.

IF IT HAS not yet set, the sliver of a moon that remains is hidden in the haze that has settled over the water. It's just after midnight and we're about fifty miles off the coast of Spain. Chris has gone down to sleep and I'm alone in the cockpit, watching a light off our port bow — a fishing boat? a tuna net?

It's a fishing boat, I decide. Unless tuna nets move around, which I don't think they do. And there's another one. I'll have to keep a close eye on them — the fishermen are way too busy with their nets to notice a pesky sailboat, never mind alter course to avoid it.

It's almost too hazy to see the stars, but I know they're up there. I'm going to miss the night sky. I never get tired of it. And I'm going to miss this boat, my little galley, all the gleaming wood below, and the comfortable leather couches, the brass lamp swinging overhead. Our little berth, which feels smaller and smaller as Bica grows. We are heading home with a five-month old puppy, a little ball of brown curls nestled in beside me on the cockpit bench.

What will Bica make of living on land? The boat is the only home she's known.

WE CELEBRATED MY fiftieth birthday in fine style in Palma de Mallorca. Chris took me out for a nice dinner, and I kept expecting him to present me with a little box. Mallorca is famous for its pearls, not natural pearls, not cultivated pearls, but not plastic pearls, either. They manufacture pearls, somehow. I had seen them in all the shop windows. They were lovely. So I was surprised when, as we lingered over the last of our bottle of wine, he pulled a photograph out of his pocket.

"Your birthday present," he said.

It was a picture of a puppy with brown curly hair and white paws. My heart leapt. A puppy! I missed Emily so much, I pined for her, Chris knew that. He'd watched me go up to strangers and pet their dogs. Leaving her behind was the hardest thing I'd ever done. Emily lived with us on the boat for a while before we set out into the ocean, but we found out the hard way that she couldn't swim. Some bulldogs can, but not Emily. She sank like a stone, head first, straight to the bottom. Chris had to rescue her more than once. And she cried when we were under sail, hated the motion of the boat. I think she was just too old to adjust to this new life.

Chris knew what I was thinking.

"This puppy is going to do just fine on the boat," he said. "She's a Spanish water dog. She's too young to leave her mother just yet — in July we'll sail to the mainland to pick her up, in Cartagena."

I gazed into her milky blue eyes. She stared boldy back at me. Come on! Let's go! I loved her already. But as I studied her picture, my heart sank. She'll break my heart. All puppies do. Am I strong enough to go through that again?

We decided to call her Bica, the word for the Portuguese version of espresso we came to love during our winter in Portimão. She's coffee-coloured and has the boundless energy of someone who has dashed back one too many bica. When she's awake, that is. She sleeps much of the time. Her favourite spot is wedged under the dinghy on the foredeck, where she's out of the sun.

Having Bica on board changed everything — for better and for worse.

The day we picked her up, we took the spinnaker ashore to refold it. I had her on her leash, which I'd slipped through one of my belt loops, leaving both hands free for me to work.

"Why don't you let her go, see what she does?" Chris said, reaching over and unsnapping the leash from her collar.

"Please don't!" There was an edge of panic, of desperation in my voice. All I could see was this little ball of brown curls tumbling into the dark, choppy waters of the harbour. He picked her up, angrier than I'd ever seen him, shoved her roughly into my hands and walked away. I felt stunned, and sick at heart.

I took her below, put her in the little bed I'd made for her at the foot of the V-berth, slumped on the settee feeling utterly hopeless.

Bica peered at me from the safety of her little nest. Then she hopped over the barricade and sprawled on the floor at my feet.

Things were pretty cool between us as we left Cartagena a few days later with our little puppy on board and sailed back to the Balearics. We had decided to anchor for a while in a sheltered harbour we had found near the town of Andratx on the southwest tip of Majorca, to make this our home base for a few weeks while Bica got used to living on a boat. And we got used to her.

She taught us a lot about the sun, our little Spaniard. She simply would not go out in the middle of the day, would run from patch of shade to patch of shade if we tried to make her walk somewhere. The Mediterranean sun is a sneaky thing. There's always a nice steady sea breeze, so you don't realize how hot it is until you have a splitting headache. We started taking a siesta during the hottest part of the day, just like Bica—not under the dinghy, though.

My fear of her falling in the water began to ease after Chris and I took her to a sheltered beach to teach her how to swim. I left her on shore with him and waded out, intending to coax her into the water. But when I turned around, there she was, swimming happily behind me. I guided her to shore, and when her feet touched bottom, she scampered up on the beach and ran around like a crazy thing, barking and tripping over her own feet. Then she ran back into the water for more. Clearly she was born knowing how to swim.

I still liked to keep her in the cockpit unless one of us was above deck to keep an eye on her. She was so small. I feared that if she went overboard, we would have trouble finding her little brown head in the water. With her curls slicked down, she was no bigger than a rat. Bica and I would play tapas bar. She would stand on her hind legs with her paws on the sill of the companionway—she could just reach—and I would put little treats on the ledge for her—tiny pieces of cheese, little bits of sausage.

Chris liked to let her run free on the deck. When he played with her, I would go below and do chores or read, listen to her little feet scampering on the deck above my head. I began to think maybe he was right: Maybe it was almost impossible for a creature with four legs who was only ten inches tall to fall over a four-inch scupper.

One evening, as we were stretched out on the foredeck enjoying the gentle breeze, Bica stretched out beside us on the cool steel deck, Chis apologized for getting so angry with me the day Bica came on board.

"I was never allowed do anything risky with the kids," he explained. "I wasn't allowed to take them in the water when there was a big surf. I wasn't allowed to take them flying with me. I wasn't really allowed to take them with me on my motorcycle. But I did."

"More wine?"

Chris refills our glasses.

"I didn't handle that very well, either," I admitted, taking a sip. "All I want is for her to be safe."

"All I want is for her to be free."

I look up at him, smile gently.

"We're not talking about the puppy here, are we?"

BICA IS SLEEPING soundly on the bench beside me. Every now and then I reach over and touch her brown curls. She grumbles in her sleep but tolerates this: it's something humans seem to need to do. The other night I was idly watching the phosphorescence that trails behind the boat when I realized that there was something on the stern deck, hmm, looks like… a puppy! It was Bica. She had hopped out one of the back windows (I didn't know she could do that) and was just enjoying the night air, watching the wake stretch out behind us. Ever since, I like to check from time to time and make sure she's still in the cockpit.

She is. And there are no boats in sight, no sails to tend. And another two hours before my watch is over. This would be a good time to write one last letter to Brenda. I go below and as quietly as I can, pull my computer out of the locker.

Dear Brenda,

It's a warm, windless night and we're motoring relentlessly over glassy seas towards Lagos and our flight home. I think we've entered Portuguese waters—a few minutes ago I heard the unmistakable sound of Portuguese on the radio, a fishing boat, probably, but I don't see any lights and the radar isn't picking anything up, so it must be pretty far away. And may it stay there. I want to enjoy this last bit of peace and quiet.

We will be in Lagos by tomorrow evening, so this is my last night watch for a very long time. And probably my last chance to write to you before I see you at the airport. When we get to the boatyard, we'll be working full out to get the boat decommissioned before our flight home.

I'm going to miss these night watches, Beek. There's something about the darkness, about being alone with the stars. Something expands in me, I feel like there's enough room for me out here. And I love this life.

Our last morning at anchor in the Med, I was in my tiny galley, emptying our last bag of chickpeas into a plastic jar that fits exactly into the little shelf behind the stove while I waited for the kettle to boil. Chris was at the nav station—you're supposed to spread charts out on the nav station, determine headings using parallel rulers, calculate magnetic variance, and so on—but he had his voltmeter out, and some tiny screws, and was working away at something, I don't know what, but from time to time the meter would beep. Bica was sprawled out on the floor at the bottom of the companionway ladder, chewing happily on a rawhide bone, and suddenly I was washed with happiness.

This is my life, I thought, this hot, sunny Tuesday morning bobbing gently at anchor somewhere along the Costa del Sol. I looked out my tiny window, watched the waves lapping the sand beach at the base of a chalky cliff. A tern plunged into the water beside the boat, came up with a silvery fish, flew away, a couple of noisy gulls in pursuit.

I wonder what it will be like to live in a tiny apartment, that's all we'll be able to afford. To get up and go to work every day. Do normal things on the weekend, go grocery shopping, get the oil changed in the car. A car. We'll have to get a car. Chris will need it for his work. I'll have to get some work clothes. I gave all mine away. So will he. And neither of us has a winter coat, or boots.

We've never lived together except on the boat. He'll have nothing to tinker with. I can see myself coming home from work and finding the kitchen sink in pieces, the television taken apart.

"Look, you can turn the taps on and off with the remote now!"

"Are you worried about going home?" I asked Chris before he went down to sleep after supper.

"A little."

When Chris admits to being a little worried, I know he is a lot worried.

And so am I.

I think you'll find me much changed, Beek. I've crossed an ocean, survived not one but two proper North Atlantic gales, and I feel so proud, so sure of myself now. But it's more than just a sense of physical accomplishment. I feel at home, some-how. We say we're heading home, but what if home isn't a place? What if it's a feeling? Maybe you can feel at home anywhere.

As we were making our way back along the Mediterranean coast of Spain, we anchored for a night in a little cove below the ruins of a castle. We figured we'd have the place to ourselves — the pilot guide described it as an imposing anchorage with fluky winds, and sure enough, we were the only boat there.

But as I scanned the shore, I realized we were not alone. There was the castle, and there was narrow sand beach, and there was... a naked person walking along the shore. The cove is only accessible by foot — it's part of a national park, and there are no roads leading to it, so we didn't really expect to find any people there. But as I looked more closely, I could make out a number of dwellings on the hillside behind the beach, caves and other rough shelters in the rubble below the castle. And a number of naked people. I quickly lowered my binoculars.

In time, we worked up the courage to go ashore. We didn't bother to lock the dinghy to a tree—where exactly would a naked person in a stolen dinghy go? Feeling somewhat over-dressed, we strolled as casually as we could across the sand to the path leading up to the castle.

Away from the beach, we discovered that many but not all of the people wore clothes. Most of them wore rough shoes of some description, handmade, for the most part. One woman was wearing a white long-sleeved shirt. Another had tied a fringed scarf around her waist. We passed a man wearing nothing but a pair of sandals and a straw hat (where do you look?).

It wasn't at all clear which of the many paths lead to the castle. As we stood at a junction trying to decide which way to go, a man—clothed, thank goodness, and carrying a plastic water jug—approached us.

"Hello," he said. He was the first person to acknowledge our presence, never mind speak to us.

"Hello," Chris said. We were both surprised that he spoke English. "Is this the way to the castle?"

"Yes, yes. It's just up here." He motioned for us to follow him. "You're from Canada. Did you sail across?" Clearly our presence in the harbour had been noted.

"Yes," Chris answered.

"I've made that trip many times. I used to be with Greenpeace, on the *Rainbow Warrior*."

Is that how you lost your arm, I wanted to ask him, but we'd arrived at a clearing where a group of people had gathered around a little spring. Water dribbled through a small opening in the rocks, splashed down into a stone basin. Someone had carved a woman's head out of stone and placed it above the spring. I wanted to take a picture of it, but was too shy to get out the camera.

"Don't go in the tower," the man from Greenpeace called after us as we continued along the path. "It's not safe."

On our way back to the boat, he waved to us from his cave above the path.

"Come for tapas!"

Chris was climbing the path before I could think of a reason not to. Banana pancakes, he and his partner offered us. And tea. All carried in over the mountains. I felt bad about using up any of their provisions, but they were happy to have us there. As the sun disappeared behind the mountains, the man's partner went inside and came out wearing a buckskin jacket. Only a buckskin jacket. But by now it didn't seem strange to be sipping tea with a man who had no pants on. I could live here, I thought, among these naked cave dwellers.

I've been listening to Ladysmith on this watch (*homeless, homeless, moonlight shining on a midnight lake*), looking up at the stars, hoping, as always, to see a falling star. I find myself thinking about how we are all homeless, in a way. I could live anywhere now, I think.

But I'll admit I'm looking forward to coming back to Canada for a while. It will feel good, I think, to put the boat on the hard, empty out all the cupboards, change the oil... (believe me, you don't want to hear the whole list.) I'm looking forward to sleeping in a real bed again (so much room!) To getting our bikes back, going to the market on Saturday mornings and buying cuts of meat I can recognize, vegetables I know how to cook. To walking in familiar woods again (with Bica!), to going to plays in English, and movies again. To cooking on a real stove, with four burners that don't run out of fuel, and a big oven. To soaking in a bath until the water runs cold.

I should be seeing shore lights soon. Only forty-five minutes left on my watch. Breakfast. I'm thinking about breakfast. A big bowl of bran flakes with a banana sliced on top. A cup of coffee with Chris while the sun comes up. Then a long nap.

See you in just two weeks, Beek. I can't wait to see your face. Thanks for offering to pick us up at the airport. You shouldn't have any trouble spotting us in the crowd. We'll be the couple in serious need of haircuts, wearing scruffy jeans and faded shirts and carrying a dog crate. A regular little family, Chris says. It's like coming back from our honeymoon with a two-year-old.

Love,
Linda

IT'S GOOD TO be busy—leaves me no time to think about going home—and the boatyard in Lagos is a good place to be busy—everyone is. The whine of the travel lift wakes us every morning, then the steady thrum of the pressure washer as they blast barnacles off the bottoms of boats. A crew is painting the hull of the boat beside us, their portable radio on full volume, pop tunes from a decade ago. I'm not sure if they know what the words mean, but they know them all.

"My name is Luka," they belt out cheerfully. "Just don't ask me how I am."

They're not sure what to make of us, doing our own boat work. Most people leave their boats here and head home while decks are replaced, hulls painted, new rigging installed. But we're doing everything ourselves. We remove the sails, wash the salt off them, spread them out on the pavement to dry, then fold them neatly and stow them in the V-berth. We soak our lines in pails, hang them on the fence in the sun. We pull all of the chain out of the anchor locker, hose it down before re-stowing it.

We haven't had the boat out of the water in a long time. It looks strange up on boat stands, balancing on its keel. We inspect every inch of the hull, check the zincs, the prop. Except for a few tenacious barnacles in some of the through-hulls, things are looking pretty good. We spend several days sanding and painting the bottom, hard work, but satisfying.

At six o'clock the workers go home and we have the boatyard to ourselves. We hit the showers, then sit on deck with a cold beer and watch the fishermen come in after a long day out on the water. The big boats seem to do okay, but the men in small open boats sometimes come home empty-handed. No wonder the men in the boatyard seem so happy. At least they can feed their families. We fall into bed before it gets dark, exhausted, then are wakened by the travel lift at first light.

I empty all the food lockers, wonder how on earth we're going to consume eight cans of tuna, two jars of capers, one jar of spaghetti sauce, two jars of peanut butter, and a can of artichokes in the next couple of weeks, never mind the many pounds of rice and pasta and dried beans. I agonize over what to take with me, what to leave behind. My olive bowls? The skimpy sundress and gold espadrilles I bought in Mallorca? Will I wear them in Canada?

Some things require no thought: I'll take my recipe for paella and several packets of saffron. The little pink top I bought in St. Martin will stay on the boat, along with the long white cotton skirt I picked up in Antigua. The backgammon board and a nice bottle of port will stay behind as well, so that when we come back to check on the boat, as we will have to do from time to time until we can get back to it for good, it will feel like home.

THREE DAYS TO go. We've rinsed the decks with fresh water, flushed and serviced the engine, topped up the batteries, put additive in the fuel to keep it from growing things while we're away. The water tanks are empty and disinfected, the bilges are clean and dry. The fridge is almost empty, too, and we're down to two tins of tuna and a can of artichokes. We're pretty much ready.

And then the unthinkable happens.

Chris is heading to the shower. I'm down below, making coffee, and Bica is sitting on the deck watching him go, as she's done every morning we've been in the boatyard. But for whatever reason, this time she decides she's going with him and flings herself over the side. We are twelve feet above the ground, which is solid asphalt.

Chris hears a thud, followed by a heart-wrenching scream. I fly up the steps of the companionway to find him carrying a limp, crying puppy up the ladder. We're too stunned to say a word to each other.

As luck would have it, we have the number for an emergency vet at hand—there's one on the tourist map of the town. While Chris covers her with a blanket and tries to comfort her, I dial the number. A sleepy vet asks all the important questions. Is she bleeding? Are there any broken bones? No and no. Or at least none that we can see. She won't let us touch her right leg. The vet provides directions to the clinic and tells us she'll meet us there.

Next problem: the clinic is in the next village and we have no car. I hurry across the river and dash from rental place to rental place until I find someone with a car available. I rush through the paperwork, grab the keys, run out into the street. The car is wedged impossibly between two other cars. I run back into the rental place.

"Get my car out for me. Now!"

Bossy American, I'm sure they're thinking. I race back to the boatyard. Chris is waiting at the gate with Bica, who is now quiet and shaking but alert, still wrapped in her blanket.

How can a puppy survive such a fall? I think as we drive away. Surely she is all smashed up inside. I put these thoughts from my mind and concentrate on finding the clinic—no easy task. The next village is full of narrow streets and dead ends. At last we find the place. The vet is there, waiting. She takes us right in.

"Can she walk?"

We don't know. The vet tells Chris to set her on the ground, then step away and call her. I've never seen anything as heart-wrenching as our little puppy, hobbling across the floor on three legs, crying out as she goes. All she wants is to be back in Chris's arms. Clearly three of her legs are just fine. But the fourth... The vet tells us she needs to x-ray her back right leg and hip, tells us we had better wait outside.

A half hour later—a long half hour later—the vet comes out. Bica has a plastic cast on her leg. Broken in three places, the vet tells us. And she may have injured her bladder—a very common thing when puppies have had a great fall. We are to give her pills to keep her sedated, and if she doesn't pee in the next few hours, we're to bring her back.

We take her home, cuddle up with her in the cockpit, and just pet her and watch her. She falls fast asleep, no longer in pain, thank goodness. Then she wakes and, wonder of wonders, wants to pee. Chris carries her carefully to the aft deck, helps her stand. She squats awkwardly in her plastic cast and a beautiful puddle of clear yellow urine appears.

"Puppies can't fly," I murmur to her as she falls back to sleep in my arms.

"I'll make some coffee," Chris says.

We know we should be working. We still have a lot to do in the now only two days left. But all I want to do is sit in the cockpit and hold our puppy while she sleeps. Chris goes below and I stroke her curly head.

Chris emerges with two steaming cups of coffee, sets them on the side benches to cool. A fishing boat has come in with its catch, a flock of gulls trailing behind, crying loudly. We watch them scrapping over bits of fish floating in the water. Carefully, without disturbing Bica, Chris pulls me close to him.

"I don't want to go back," he says.

"Neither do I."

The boatyard is quiet now, most of the workers gone home for the day. But the sun won't set for another couple of hours. We should get back to work. But instead we sit quietly in the cockpit, the three of us, until the sun begins to set.

I have come to truly love this sturdy boat, I think, surveying the rust patches that show us every nick in the paint, now that we've been in salt water. The varnish that's fading and in some places peeling after a winter in the tropical sun. The makeshift preventers we've rigged. The teak deck, silver now after being scoured by the seas.

And I have come to love this man more than I thought possible. I promised I would never put myself in the way of another broken heart, but here I am. I trust this man. I trust this boat. And I realize that I trust myself, in a way I never have before.

IT'S TIME TO go. We have clearance from the vet to travel with our broken puppy, who is already putting a little weight on her leg. She's going to be okay. But are we? We open up the bilge so it can air while we're away, lock up the boat, tarp it as best we can to protect it from the sun and rain.

I look back as we drive away. The bow of the boat hangs over the boatyard fence. Our anchor is the last thing I see.

*Postscript: I'll fly away*

We've been back in Canada almost a full week before I manage to slip away from Brenda's place in Guelph for a walk along the river. Bica still can't walk far with her cast and Chris has stayed behind to keep an eye on her. It feels funny to be out on my own.

It's a beautiful sunny day, cool, fresh. The leaves are just starting to turn. I hear a kingfisher scolding loudly, see a flash of blue as he skims across the dam, disappears into a maple tree on the other side of the river. There is a rustle in the leaves above my head. A flock of cedar waxwings is working the elderberry bushes beside the path. There are still berries on them. Enough to make a pie for Thanksgiving? I inspect the bushes closely. Not quite.

A young woman with a golden retriever puppy comes around the bend. I struggle for the right words. *Ola? Buenos dias? Bom dia?*

"Good morning," she says, with a smile.

Oh, yeah.

"Good morning," I reply.

> *Chris and I are in the Azores, walking along a winding road lined with purple hydrangeas. We're lost, of course. We come to a little village. There's an old woman dressed in black leaning on the low stone wall in front of her house. She looks sad and tired, her face lined with years of toil and worry.*
>
> *"Bom dia," I say, then because I'm Canadian, I begin my question with "Desculpe…" The words come to me slowly. "Onde está, um…"*
>
> *She breaks into a wide grin, all trace of sternness disappears completely from her face.*

*"The caldera is just up this road," she says in perfect
English. "Turn right at the next crossroads."*
*How many times a day does she say this? Is this the
only English she knows, or is she perfectly bilingual?
I'm embarrassed by my limited Portuguese.*
*"Muito obrigada," I say.*
*"Nada."*

Everything will be easier here in Canada, with no language barriers to contend with.

And harder.

I FIND A job at the university and Chris starts looking for work. We rent a small apartment on campus — people comment on how tiny our place is, but it's huge compared with the boat. We get the few things we have out of storage, hang up our favourite picture: a tall ship out on the open sea, crashing through the waves, a small figure in yellow foul-weather gear on the foredeck, hanging onto the rigging for dear life.

Before we left, I had said to Chris, "We'll never see seas like that, right?" Now we look at the picture and smile. We've been through much worse.

Several trips to IKEA later, we've furnished our apartment with bookshelves and tables and chairs that will break down and store flat when we go back to the boat. In a year, we're thinking. We should be able to get back to the boat in a year. Next time, we've decided, we're going to keep a household in storage, just in case.

We set up a tiny office for Chris in the corner of the living/dining/kitchen area of our 400-square-foot space. Bica claims the armchair beside his desk as her domain, sleeps there curled up in a ball while he works. Barks at him when she wants to go out and play. Chris has decided to take advantage of living on campus and has signed up for a few graduate courses. Not surprisingly, he's particularly interested in corrosion. And alternative energy sources.

I unpack my books, my *Gashlycrumb Tinies*! I curl up on the couch, flip through the pages. There's Neville, still peering out the window. And Prue, still reaching for the door handle. Don't do it! I want to tell her. Then I think, maybe Neville doesn't die of ennui after all. Maybe he's just waiting for the rain to stop so he can go outside and play. And maybe Prue isn't actually trampled to death, maybe she gets up and brushes herself off, a little wiser about the ways of the world.

I DISCOVER THAT things in the workplace have changed in the five years I've been away. There is so much to learn — the university has moved to an online calendar system called BookIt. It takes me a while to get used to the idea that people can just book me whenever they feel like it, but I can book them too. It's kind of fun.

There are other new realities to get used to. The puzzling signs in all the washrooms. I study a picture of a man sneezing violently into his elbow. I thought sneezing was something people pretty much knew how to do. WASH YOUR HANDS, another sign orders. In case you're not sure how to do this, step-by-step instructions are provided. In the supply cupboard, along with a giddying array of pens and Post-it notes and pads of paper, there is some kind of killer antibacterial product for wiping down door handles and phones NOT TO BE USED BY PREGNANT WOMEN. What is going on here? I discover that the university has a pandemic plan.

Before long, I'm booking meetings online, sneezing into my elbow, and washing my hands like a pro. It feels like I never left.

Sometimes, though, when I'm in a meeting, my mind drifts. Instead of concentrating on how to enrich the work-term experience of junior co-op students, I find myself thinking about the young girl who used to slink into the café in Portimão where I liked to go to write letters. She would sidle up to a table, grimy palm outstretched, dark eyes imploring. The tourists would wave her off, embarrassed, but the locals would take her up to the counter, let her pick out a small cake, which the woman behind the counter would wrap up for her. One day I saw the girl out on the street, sharing her cake with the tiny, wrinkled woman who sold chestnuts in the square—her mother? her grandmother? The old woman was hungry.

There are worse things than spending your first co-op work term filing sewage plans.

ONE AFTERNOON I find myself standing in front of a big map of the world on the wall outside the office of the associate dean in charge of international agreements. With my finger, I trace a line down the Erie Canal to the Hudson River, past New York City to the ocean, down the coast of the United States to Miami, then across the Gulf Stream to the Bahamas. That's farther than most people sail in a lifetime. But my finger keeps moving, farther south to Antigua, then a long arc from Antigua up toward Bermuda, then across a wide expanse of open sea to the Azores.

It's a big ocean. We sailed across it. Twenty-six days, it took us. I'm not the same person I was before.

SATURDAY MORNING I make the rounds, to Vincenzo's for cheese and olives and bread, to the florist on Belmont for a spray of yellow freesia, to the Old Kitchen Cupboard for the makings of a big batch of granola. I'm thrilled to have a full-sized oven again. I'm baking cakes and cookies, even soufflés again, things that are hard to make when the only temperatures available to you are zero and 400.

I'm scooping rolled oats into a plastic bag when I spot a big glass jar filled with dried figs. I stop what I'm doing, study them. They look so pale and shrivelled. I know now that fresh figs are a beautiful deep purple. And these miserable things are more than $12 a pound. I can't believe my eyes.

> *We're clambering around the ruins of the old fort on the island of Menorca. We come across a huge bush spilling over an old stone wall and down the hillside towards the sea. It's heavy with figs.*

*It takes us a while to figure out how to pick them. You can't just pull them off the bush or you end up with squashed figs and purple hands. You have to hold the ripe fruit in the palm of your hand, then twist it gently until the stem gives away. We fill our pockets with them, then our hats, then our hands, as many as we can carry. They are warm from the sun.*

*We take them back to the boat and I slice them in half, cover them with a crumble topping, bake them in my little oven. That's our supper. We eat huge bowls of warm fig crisp drizzled with cream, wash it down with a bottle of Spanish wine as we watch the sun go down behind the island, listen to the gulls settling on the rocky cliffs for the night.*

I'M PEDALLING AS hard as I can to keep up with Chris, those long legs of his, but so far, I'm doing okay. Perhaps having Bica in a bike trailer behind him slows him down just enough. I can see her little brown head through the back window — she's loving this. It's the fastest she's gone since she broke her leg.

We're on our way to the Waterloo farmers' market, a good fifteen-kilometre bike ride. It's been a long, cold winter and we're both glad to be outside again, heading off on a little adventure. Will there be asparagus at the market? For sure there will be rhubarb by now. I'll make us a pie.

Summer sausage. Chris is probably thinking about summer sausage.

I'm keeping an eye out for lilacs along the way, planning to swipe a few branches on the way home. I scan the ditches for wild garlic. Then remember where I am.

This being home is okay, though. We've settled happily into our little apartment, and we're finding it a relief not to have to worry about dragging anchor in the night. Every morning we wake up in exactly the same place we went to sleep.

I've discovered that I can do my job—in fact, I'm rather good at it. I've made peace with pantyhose, have a smart haircut again, and I like my new work clothes. And Chris is enjoying his work and his studies. I see a wind turbine in our future, to supplement the solar panels on the boat.

Oops, I'm falling behind. I pedal like mad on a downhill stretch to make up the distance. We stop at the top of the next hill, to catch our breath and have a swig of water. I take off my helmet, run my fingers through my hair. The sun is warm on my face.

Bica whines to get going. We both smile. Such a little tyrant.

This is nice, I think, as we don our helmets and pedal off again.

BRENDA IS DRIVING me back to Waterloo after a day of shopping for summer work clothes. There's been a big accident on Highway 7, so we're taking the back way. Anna is in her booster seat in the back. She's looking out the window, swinging her feet, kicking the back of Brenda's seat from time to time.

"Anna," Brenda warns her. She stops for a minute, then starts swinging her feet again.

"Can we sing, Mama?" she asks.

Brenda pushes a CD into the player, fast-forwards without looking to the song she wants.

> *Some glad morning when this life is o'er*
> *I'll fly away*
> *To a home on God's celestial shore*
> *I'll fly away*

Anna knows all the words, and her voice is sweet and strong and true. I had no idea she could sing like this. This is something that has happened while I was away. I glance over at Brenda. She's smiling, listening to her daughter sing. My sister's hair, which was black when I left, is touched with grey now, and there are more lines around her eyes than I remember. But she looks happy.

"You guys sing the other part," Anna orders when she reaches the chorus. She doesn't know that Brenda and I have been singing together since we were kids. This is one of our favourite songs. Brenda picks out the harmony above the line Anna is singing. I fall in below. As our voices intertwine, tears fill my eyes. Brenda reaches over and takes my hand.

> *I'll fly away O glory*
> *I'll fly away in the morning*
> *When I die, Hallelujah, by and by*
> *I'll fly away...*

I squeeze Brenda's hand. We'll fly back to Portugal, Chris and I, as soon as we can, and pick up where we left off. But this is home for now, and this moment feels as heavy and sweet as a ripe fig.

## Acknowledgements

I am deeply indebted to Alice Munro for showing me—and the world—that the lives of girls and women matter. Her work makes my story possible.

Writing this book was a journey no less fraught with peril for me than crossing the ocean, and I thank the people who were brave enough to accompany me. Mick and Jenny Cooper and my sister Sandy Kenyon read each chapter as I completed it and looked forward to the next. Dejan Ristic walked the beach on Toronto Island with me each morning, our dogs trotting along behind, and listened to me complain about how hard writing is, then sent me back to my computer.

Ann Vanderhoof provided me with invaluable advice on my first draft (what do you mean, narrative arc?) and encouraged me to work with Allyson Latta, whose coaching helped shape this book.

In a literary world drowning in memoir, I am grateful to Karen Haughian of Signature Editions for her enthusiastic response to my manuscript and for believing that there was enough sea room out there for one more little boat.

This book would not have been possible without Judith Miller's unfailing belief in this project and the constant support of Charlene Diehl, my friend, my lifeline. My sister Brenda Kenyon read every draft and pushed me to dig deeper. Without her, this book would have been just another tale of adventure on the high seas.

My deepest debt is to Chris Hatton, my love, my life, my constant companion, on this and every journey, big and small. Thank you for taking me out there. And for bringing me back in one piece.

*About the author*

Linda Kenyon is a Canadian writer who lives year-round with her husband Chris Hatton on one boat or another—either their forty-three-foot steel sailboat, currently in the Bahamas, or the boat they built in a meadow on their farm south of Owen Sound, Ontario.

Stories about their sailing adventures appear regularly in magazines and Linda has had many short stories published in Canadian literary journals. She has written two books of flash fiction, *You Are Here*, published by Trout Lily Press, and *This is a love song, sort of,* published by Stonegarden Studios, as well as a book of nonfiction, *Rainforest Bird Rescue: Changing the future for endangered wildlife*, published by Firefly Books, which won a Science in Society Journalism Award from the Canadian Science Writers Association.

Visit her at lindakenyon.ca.